To Jan —
with best wishes on
your book.

YOU'VE GOT THE TIME

Ken Wachsberger

Ken Wachsberg

YOU'VE GOT THE TIME

How to Write and Publish That Book in You

2nd edition

by

Ken Wachsberger

Published by
Azenphony Press, 2024

Published by

Azenphony Press
PO Box 130884
Ann Arbor, MI 48113-0884
U.S.A.
info@azenphonypress.com
(734) 635-0577

You've Got the Time: How to Write and Publish That Book in You, 2nd ed.
Copyright February 8, 2024 by Ken Wachsberger
ISBN 978-0-945531-20-3 (ebook)
ISBN 978-0-945531-21-0 (pbk)
ISBN 978-0-945531-22-7 (hbk)

Cover by Caligraphics
http://www.caligraphics.net

What others are saying about Ken and
YOU'VE GOT THE TIME:
HOW TO WRITE AND PUBLISH THAT BOOK IN YOU

"Wow, Ken. The teachings within your book are Great…. Thanks and God bless you."
—Floyd Wickman, Hall of Fame Member of the National Speakers Association

'One of the most 'user friendly' and comprehensive how-to manuals for writers seeking publication of their work…."
–*Midwest Book Review*

"If any of you are writing a book, go out and get yourself a Ken right away! He held my hand through the doubts and fears, pulled me out of the stuck places, and turned me into a writing ninja!"
—Kristi Lynn Davis, *Long Legs and Tall Tales: A Showgirl's Wacky, Sexy Journey to the Playboy Mansion and the Radio City Rockettes*

"Ken Wachsberger is an amazing editor, AND he's a member of National Speakers Association so he understands speakers. Ken edited my latest book, and I was thoroughly pleased with his work. I'll be sending many of my book coaching clients to Ken!"
— Cathy Fyock, *The Speaker Author: Sell More Books and Book More Speeches*

"If you want a book that other people want to read, you need to talk to Ken…. What he was able to do was actually find my voice and … make it even more me…. [E]veryone who reads it now says they can hear me talking."
— Greg Peters, *Hello and a Handshake: The Reluctant Networker's Guide to Survival and Success at Your Next Business Gathering*

"Your new book is my bedtime reading – terrific read, like you are there talking to me – you covered it all, fabulous."
–Perley-Ann Friedman, *Volunteer Fundraising Simplified*

"Don't hire Ken! Unless you want impeccable editing skills. He's the best!"
— Kathryn Dempsey, *SHED HAPPENS! 7 Ways to Overcome Life's Challenges at Work & Life*

"And don't even think of signing a book contract before you read the section on contracts; Ken is also a contract adviser with the National Writers Union."
—Susan Schopp, historian, member, National Writers Union, author, *Sino-French Trade at Canton, 1698-1842*

DEDICATION

To Emily, who has always been my Jennifer

TABLE OF CONTENTS

The big reward is your finished book. Short-term rewards along the way give you the boost to get there.

You can deepen your bonds with your loved ones as you approach the finish line even as your book starts sucking up your family time. And it will.

The author praises the power of words and recalls his victory over the city of Syracuse with a series of forceful letters.

FOREWORD

by Sheryl James

It sounds like double talk, but it's true: Ken Wachsberger has written the perfect book about, well, writing books. *You've Got the Time: How to Write and Publish That Book in You* is perfect for neophyte, non-writer, I-just-wanna-write-my-book folks as well as experienced writers who somehow need more direction than their professional realms offer.

I fall into the latter category. A lifelong, successful journalist, I have written only two books, both assignments. The first was a small biography of a Michigan artist and businesswoman, requested by a small publisher; the other was an assignment from the University of Michigan Press, which was publishing a line of Michigan-themed books; my book concerned Michigan legends.

But I never have written my own book, be it an autobiography or a book full of advice about writing articles – not books – as I have done for decades.

Meanwhile, however, I have been hired to help people write their own books. I wish I had had Ken's book to help me. In every chapter, Ken offers wise, step-by-step, incredibly down-to-earth and highly detailed help for every step of the process. As experienced as I am, I find tremendous assistance here.

Perhaps the most important, foundational help this book offers is encouragement. For those who never have written, yet have in their hearts a story they want so badly to preserve and/or share, the idea of writing is intimidating at best.

Indeed, I always was embarrassed when people looked at me as some guru or magician because I was a successful journalist – as if by virtue of my awards I was somehow better than them, at least professionally.

Certainly, I am proud of what I have accomplished. But it's important to point out that I, too, was a novice once. Without the help of lots of people and a whole lot of practice, I never would have ventured into the world of journalism, or have been successful. Ken offers this kind of help to anyone who picks up this book.

Writing by its nature is arbitrary, especially for those new to this venture. The questions constantly arise: Is this a good idea? Can I write this book? Is this a good way to begin? Should I do first person or second? Is anyone going to be interested in this? And on and on.

Ken helps with all of this, and adds the even more practical advice about actually doing this task: making time, finding the right place to work, interviewing, the role of "freewriting," and identifying that perfect title (amply exemplified by his *You've Got the Time;* Ken shares how he stumbled upon this perfect title). More practical topics include indexing, the importance of qualified feedback, and self-publishing, including information about *Writer's Market* and what the National Writers Union can do for you.

There is technical advice on various computer programs, something many of us more senior writers need. Also offered is help on the all-important and all-intimidating marketing process, including utilizing such paths as the National Speakers Association; when and how to write press releases; and what the heck is Smashwords? After that, Ken addresses the minutiae of contracts; the labyrinth of copyrights, and even how writing can affect your relationships.

If you've had a longing to write your own book, be it about your life, your grandmother's life, that World War II veteran's story, your life as a self-made baker, and so on, don't wander aimlessly, wasting time and losing heart. Read this book, and let Ken hold your hand through a task he has lived many times, and has managed to decipher into a step-by-step process anyone can employ.

You've Got the Time

As if all of this isn't enough, Ken's personal style makes this not just a useful read, but a fun read as well. He shares his personal path and growth on book writing, which helps us identify all the more with him.

Thus, we can conclude, if he can do this, so can I.

Sheryl James is a Pulitzer Prize-winning journalist and the author of *The Life and Wisdom of Gwen Frostic and Michigan Legends: Folktales and Lore from the Great Lakes State*.

KEN'S INTRODUCTION
TO SECOND EDITION

by Ken

This second edition of *You've Got the Time: How to Write and Publish That Book in You* has been a long time in the works. Some chapters remain similar to the first edition, with updates to reflect constant changes in technology. Others are dramatically different and I've added four new chapters.

Smashwords Merges with Draft2Digital

The most significant changes are in the chapters regarding file production, uploading, and distribution brought about because of the merger between Smashwords and Draft2Digital (D2D) that was announced on February 8, 2022.

D2D may have been around while I was writing my first edition but I never used them and I didn't know anyone who did so I didn't even mention them. Now they were replacing Smashwords, my primary go-to platform for ebook production and distribution! I had to mention them.

The merger with Draft2Digital brought benefits to Smashwords members like me. For one, for the first time, we could create softcovers, a feat I had performed only with Amazon and IngramSpark because Smashwords didn't offer it.

Further, D2D's method of file uploading promised to be revolutionary in its simplicity and cost. Simply upload your front cover file and a Word text manuscript file and D2D will programmatically format them for softcover and ebook. They even automatically tweak your files to satisfy the idiosyncrasies of each platform.

It sounded so easy.

But I had to try out the system for myself before I could write about it.

So, I re-edited a previous book that was ready for a third edition, *Never Be Afraid: A Belgian Jew in the French Resistance*. Then I uploaded and formatted the files. I share my experience and what I learned in part four, "Publishing Your Book."

Do I Still Need Kindle?

One perk of Draft2Digital is that you can upload your files with them and your book gets distributed through their entire network of platforms including Amazon, Barnes & Noble, Kobo, Scribd, Apple, Tolino, Overdrive, Bibliotheca, 24Symbols, Baker & Taylor, Hoopla, Vivlio, and Palace Marketplace.

Since one of those platforms is Amazon, I thought, I don't need Kindle to get me there anymore. I considered bucking the giant and uploading only to D2D.

But I confronted an issue that you will confront also if you have already distributed your book on Amazon and now are writing a new edition: What happens to your reviews when you change your ISBN? Also in part four, I show you how to distribute a new edition of your book on Amazon and D2D without losing the reviews you got from your earlier edition on Amazon and without, believe it or not, having to get a second ISBN for the same format.

National Writers Union Splits with UAW

In a long-overdue move, the National Writers Union split from its affiliation as a chapter within the United Auto Workers. The announcement was made in a joint press release from leaders of both unions on April 30, 2020, effective May 11.

NWU affiliated with UAW in 1992 as UAW Local 1981 of the AFL-CIO, with a plan of action that sounded good on paper but was never successfully implemented, a topic for another day.

You've Got the Time

But the contract advising and grievance work that has attracted members since 1981, when the National Writers Union was founded (hence, Local 1981), is still one of the union's most valuable member benefits. I've been a contract adviser for nearly forty years, with my specialty area being academic press contracts, which are among the worst in the business.

This second edition. makes no mention of UAW or Local 1981.

Cost to Copyright

At the same time as I was preparing the first edition, Library of Congress was considering an increase in the cost to take out a copyright. A representative from LC personally concurred with me that an increase was likely but she was unable to give me specifics so I only alluded to the likelihood of an increase.

Naturally, the increase was announced soon after my release date. I updated the chapter in a blog and carry that update now into this second edition. May the Library of Congress give me a few years to be correct before making any additional increases.

Other Changes

Many more. Join me inside.

KEN'S INTRODUCTION
TO FIRST EDITION

by Ken

Writing a book is a way of life, tasks woven into unrelated acts and scenarios throughout the day, not merely an hour-a-day routine. You may think you don't have the time to write a book but you do. You just have to find the cracks of unscheduled moments in your day and make the best use of them.

Helping You Become a Better Writer

In this book I will help you to discover those unscheduled moments so you never again have to say, "I don't have time." I will teach you how to write a better nonfiction book faster with less stress by preparing your mindset to be a writer and sharing a few tricks of the trade:

- I'll talk about writing as a nonlinear process and teach you how to create order out of the thoughts and ideas already swirling around chaotically in your mind. You don't have to write chapter one first and then chapter two. Your book will have a table of contents but it may only materialize after any number of chapters have been written, in a random order you probably will never be able to recreate — or care to.

- I'll teach you how to name what will otherwise become an overwhelming folder of electronic files — including chapter and manuscript drafts, web text, freewriting adventures, and your vast network of correspondence that will include typesetters, artists, printers, web developers, editors, experts, celebrities, and many others — so you can find them when you need them.

- Experts and celebrities to write those forewords and testimonials that will give your book credibility and marketability? I'll help you locate them and reach out to them with well-crafted email invitations. Why settle for less?

- Don't ever think you can't write a book because you're no good at mechanics, grammar, and spelling. I'll help you overcome that fallacy while teaching you the joy of deleting so you never settle for a manuscript that is "good enough."

- I'll teach you how to prepare for and conduct expert interviews so you can sound like an authority even when you know you aren't one.

- I'll encourage you to look into audiobook production before you put away your ISBN sheet.

- I'll share ideas of my own and from masters of book marketing that will help you increase your book promotion and sales.

And much more.

Most of my early teaching and coaching work I did with students and clients who had little if any writing experience and were bewildered by the process. Some of the chapters in this book are directed to writers like them.

Should you publish through an established publishing company or create your own company and publish it yourself? I will discuss pros and cons of going both ways. The answer will be largely up to you.

But if you do find yourself staring at a blank boilerplate contract from another company, you better understand what every clause means before you sign it. I'll introduce you to the National Writers Union, the only labor union for freelance writers; and share some of the secrets that I learned while advising members about book contracts for nearly four decades.

Elementary School Smart Kid

I've been in training to be a book coach and editor for most of my life. I didn't always call myself that, though.

As an elementary school smart kid, I would finish my in-class homework in five minutes and then spend the rest of the hour walking around the class answering my friends' questions one at a time.

I don't remember how that practice began. Did a friend ask me a question as I was walking to the water fountain? Did I instinctively offer to help because I would have gotten bored just sitting at my desk while everyone else worked? Or did my teacher ask me to help some kids so she could work with the other kids?

I don't have a clue. But I remember my best friend's mother, who was our class room mother, telling my mom, who was her best friend, how good I was with the other kids because I helped them and I couldn't remember ever not doing that.

I Become a Speed Writer

I became a speed writer in the fifth grade when my teacher, Mr. Brett, punished us by making us write sentences before going out to recess: "I will not talk in class. I will not talk in class." The faster you wrote, the sooner you could go outside, so you wrote fast.

I learned to write so fast I could have my ten sentences done before my classmates had their coats on. He used to devise long, convoluted sentences for me just so I wouldn't be the first one done: "I will not, whether I feel like it or not, despite the mood of my psyche or the interest level of the lecture or the temperature outside, and regardless of the liquid capacity of my bladder, talk in class."

Eventually he gave up and made me monitor. My job was to check the others to see that they did their sentences properly. He took the job away when he saw I was having too much fun.

But I gained from the experience in three ways:

1. My wrists became so limber, I became the drummer in the junior high school band.

2. I learned to write so fast that today, when I take notes at a meeting, I can transcribe what is spoken nearly verbatim without a recorder.

3. I learned, by my method of fulfilling the assignment, the principles behind mass production. Instead of writing one sentence at a time, and walking back and forth from one end of the chalkboard to the other, I would write from up to down: "I I I I I…" ten times; then "will will will…."

Transforming Lives

For over thirty years I taught writing to college students who came into my class hating writing but had to take it to graduate.

I didn't realize how powerful writing was as a tool for self-discovery until I started teaching freshman composition students at Eastern Michigan University how to write the I-Search paper, a student-friendly form of research paper that allowed them to select their own topics and present their findings in first-person journal format.

As a result, students became engulfed in their studies and wrote more than they ever believed they could write.

One student, Derek, was a horrible writer. He wouldn't be insulted if I said that to his face because he brags about how bad he used to be. The first paper he handed in to me contained every possible error in mechanics, grammar, and spelling, usually more than once. But he wrote with a passion that I seldom saw in college classes.

He wrote to find the answer to the question monopolizing his attention, how the wife of his best friend could divorce his friend and desert their daughter. By the end of the semester, he had answered many of his initial questions and had come up with others that he didn't have time to answer before his paper was due. His search continued after the semester ended.

He became a better writer in the process because he was showing off his paper to others and he didn't want it to be filled with red marks. When I saw him a year later, he announced that he considered himself a writer and so did his friends and business associates.

I had students whose lives were held captive by their dysfunctional backgrounds, where they had spent the first eighteen years of their lives getting screwed up. Now, they were living outside that environment for the first time in their lives. When they faced me for the first time, they only knew that writing and researching served no useful purpose in their lives and they hated doing it.

But writing the I-Search paper freed them from their fears and inhibitions. They looked into their own hearts and their stifled ambitions and found topics that mattered to them. Or, as Ken Macrorie, who came up with the idea of the I-Search paper, would say, the topics found them.

They wrote about a father whose alcoholism led to the break-up of the family; how to not screw up the kids any more than necessary in an impending divorce; coping with an ADD son; coming to terms with a mother's schizophrenia; coming out for the first time about being raped the year before; gay adoption; feminist art; and other topics that not only amazed me but showed the extreme courage that individuals will exhibit and the passion they will display for writing once they discover its power as a tool for self-discovery.

They also did the research necessary to publish an article in a local magazine for the first time ever, to buy a first home, a car, a car wash company, a diamond ring, and many other big-ticket items. Other students, looking forward to graduation, did career searches.

In every case, the topic wasn't "academic" in the traditional sense. In other words, they weren't forced to write twenty pages on an esoteric topic that the teacher thought was timely but had no connection to their lives.

For the first time, I heard students say, "This class changed my life." I heard it often through the quarter of a century that I taught the I-Search paper. Somewhere along the way, I wrote *Transforming Lives: A Socially Responsible Guide to the Magic of Writing and Researching,* the first textbook devoted to writing the I-Search paper.

The Ultimate Fantasy of a Writer

As a book editor, I guided contributors to one landmark series of Vietnam-era underground press insider histories through the most intense period of their lives.

During a series of interviews conducted over my kitchen table, I helped a Holocaust survivor break through forty years of repressed memories.

I've loved my life as a writer and editor. Some years I lived better than others and the professional writing I did wasn't always creative or exciting. Other times, I couldn't believe I was getting paid for it.

For seven years, I led a major project at Reveal Digital, in Saline, Michigan, to create a keyword-searchable digital collection of underground, alternative, and literary newspapers and magazines from the Civil Rights and Vietnam era, my coming-of-age years. My job was to figure out which titles to include, track down the rights holders, and obtain necessary permissions.

Most of my writing for the job was email communication but I became a master at it. In this book, I show you how you can become one, too.

I reached out to thousands of people who I located through Internet and social media research and invited them to include their publications — now crumbling and yellowing around the edges in special collections around the country — in the first-ever keyword-searchable digital collection of these publications. Hundreds responded "yes," and I created a landmark collection that will be preserved and is available online to anyone, anywhere, any time of day or night, using any search engine.

You've Got the Time

Along the way, I became an expert at Internet searching. I devised templates to communicate faster with less stress. I built a huge mailing list and constructed Excel spreadsheets to keep track of the data I was amassing.

I received invitations to speak at conferences. I wrote blog entries and gained readers. I was interviewed often. I had opportunities to promote my Voices from the Underground Series.

And I got paid for it.

That's the ultimate fantasy of a writer: to write the book you would write for nothing — and get paid for it.

My goal with this book is to help you live that fantasy.

ACKNOWLEDGMENTS

I'm grateful to many people:

Emily, David, and Carrie for inspiring me every day.

The National Speakers Association, especially the Michigan chapter, for welcoming me into your membership and embracing my services and friendship.

The National Writers Union, the premier labor union for freelance writers, brain trust of information about book contracts, and my long-time family of writers.

Geraldine Jensen, ace volunteer with SCORE, who became my business mentor and coach while I was writing this book and building my book coaching and editing business. If you don't think every great coach needs a coach, you need a coach. And hats off to SCORE, an amazing government program that brings value to the community.

Ann Hoffman, Lisa McMillan, Lisa Roach, Susan Schopp, Sue Katz, Harvey Wasserman, Dan McCrory, and brother Bob for reading and reviewing early drafts of this book and for your continued support and friendship.

Paul MacArthur, National Writers Union Assistant National Contract Adviser, for your thoughts on negotiating a book contract over the phone; and Phil Mattera, my Contract Adviser mentor.

Sheryl James, David Feldsott, Greg Peters, Dean Jeffery, Jocee Weatherly, and Steve Sharp for helping me to update technology and terminology throughout the book.

Shana Milkie, Hermina Anghelescu, Mary Peterson, David Wolf, and September Williams for introducing me to the worlds of indexing and audiobooks.

My Facebook community for helping me to update my usage of "secretary" for the twenty-first century. I've never made assumptions that the role was low status or filled by a woman. In my sample dialogue, I named my secretary Leslie. But because the term was offensive to some, I was happy to change it. I went with receptionist, which captured the mood I wanted to create and was only one word.

The good folks at every Panera I have ever visited who allow me to spend long hours in their presence even when I purchase only coffee or iced tea.

Dave Bass for helping me navigate IngramSpark with Kindle files.

Jeffrey Hayzlett, David Newman, Kristi Davis, David Dye, Mark Coker, Guy Kawasaki, Cathy Fyock, Lois Creamer, Mickie Kennedy, and Amy Jones for your ideas on book sales and promotion, website findability, and social media.

Kirk Austin, Jim Azevedo, Tara Robinett, and the Draft2Digital technology support team for your accessibility and patience.

Portions of this book first appeared in my earlier book, *Transforming Lives: A Socially Responsible Guide to the Magic of Writing and Researching.*

Apologies if I missed anyone. I can't say enough how grateful I am to all of you.

PART 1: GETTING STARTED

Post Office   KEY   stroller

Walmart return , swim shoes
Glubsironer
meat - chili + chicken
Gander
clean car
make up swim day

Hilton Garden
swim, haircut   Friday
lunch + purse

- Iron Cathy
- travel agent
visit Linda
Marilyn
Camp

Chapter 1

BASIC EQUIPMENT NEEDS

Every profession requires specific tools and equipment. For writers, so many exist to fulfill your varied needs, it could seem the hardest part about writing a book is choosing which tools and equipment best fit your lifestyle.

Something for Taking Notes

You can't be a writer if you don't take notes so let me start with your note-taking equipment. You've got options.

Tablets

Easier for note taking than laptops because they turn on with the press of a thumb, don't need to warm up, and are less intrusive in a crowded restaurant or lecture hall. They're also better for surfing the web, checking emails, and playing games.

Voice-to-text

Android and iOS devices have their versions that enable you to use voice-to-text with your notetaking apps. I used Memo on my Android until I realized I'd rather take notes in my spiral notebook. Evernote is another popular one. They record text pretty accurately but not perfectly so you need to clean up your messages. On both Android and iOS devices, you have to speak the punctuation.

Pen and Notebook

And a pen and notebook. I don't care how good technology gets. Don't ever lose the feel of pen to paper. You may not use them often because other technology is easier. But what do you do when your computer isn't around or it isn't socially acceptable for you to be on it?

- Relatives are visiting from out of town.
- You're at the theatre.
- It's shut down for the night.
- You're at your best friend's wedding.

Pens

Pens are ubiquitous. Businesses pass them out as promotions. Conference sponsors give them away to attendees as gifts along with notepads. Political campaigns tell you who to vote for on them. Keep a few in your pocket or purse at all times.

You can also get a pen that doubles as a stylus. With a stylus, you can write notes on your tablet or cell phone as easily as you would with a pen in a small notebook without removing your gloves. Technological advancements are enabling illegible handwriting to be interpreted.

Notebooks

I carry a spiral notebook with me wherever I go. They come in varying sizes. Find one that works.

For times when my notebook isn't accessible, like when I'm shopping and I leave it in the car, or I'm at the dinner table and I'm resting it by my knapsack, I carry a 3" x 5" or 4" x 6" notebook in my back pocket.

Which Method Is Right?

Don't struggle with the concept. No method is right or wrong all the time. Whatever method you use to take notes becomes an extension of your body. And your book gets done.

You've Got the Time

Laptop, Cord, Battery

Regardless of how you take notes, transfer your notes to your laptop as soon as you can. That's where you do your heavy writing.

I can't believe the freedom my laptop gives me to travel anywhere in the world for as long as I want without falling behind in my self-imposed deadlines, the deep pockets of writing time I discover tucked away in doctors' waiting rooms, airports, kids' sports games, and other precious parts of life that become on-the-road writing offices.

Get a long cord in case the closest plug is two tables away; and a strong battery in case no outlet is in sight.

Adaptors

A splitter enables you to plug in three power cords where previously only one socket was available. Splitters cost under $2 at some stores and they are indispensable for when you find the outlets already taken at the only restaurant with free Wi-Fi and your battery is approaching empty. Make friends with patrons of adjoining booths when an extra space in your splitter saves their laptop.

Other adaptors are necessary when

- You travel to Europe because products in the United States are built to run on alternating current (AC) and European products run on direct current (DC).
- You need to plug your three-prong laptop power cord into a two-prong outlet.

Microsoft Word

On my laptop, I have Microsoft Word for straight typing. Most publishers use it. The tips I'll share with you in this book are done on Microsoft Word. Macs can perform the same functions or variations so if you are a Mac user you can easily apply this information to your computer.

Google Docs is a free file-sharing program from Google's web-based Google Drive office suite that also includes Google Sheets, Google Slides, and a few others. If you routinely share your documents with multiple others, Google Docs may be easier than Word and it performs most Word functions.

Use it if you want for your book. However, before you submit your manuscript to a publisher or upload it onto your print on demand or ebook platform to publish it yourself, you'll need to convert it to Word and then check your formatting.

Backing Up Files

You've got multiple options for backing up your files. Use more than one.

USB Flash Drive

The standby has been to use a USB flash drive, also known by thumb drive, jump drive, memory stick, and multiple other names. Flash drives have so much available space nowadays, your book will not come close to using it all up even with photographs, drawings, and videos. And they're becoming even more inexpensive. You can find a good 16 gigabyte flash drive, which is way more than you'll ever need, for under $6. For the first edition of this book, I said under $10.

They are as immediate as you want them to be, and they are easy to carry around.

But, some folks warn, they are easy to lose, they will be destroyed along with everything else you own if disaster strikes your personal space, they can be corrupted, and you have to back them up manually.

The Cloud

These folks prefer the cloud because it is automatic, seamless from server to server over any Internet connection, far removed from possible onsite disaster, and increasingly more reliable than earlier versions. In addition, it liberates information technology departments from the task of maintaining backup and storage.

You've Got the Time

With the cloud, you can, depending on the services provided by your plan:

- Back up data continuously or at pre-arranged times, on all devices, operating systems, and platforms.
- Store unlimited data, including files of any size.
- Retrieve lost files through digital download, on an external hard drive, or on a USB flash drive.

In addition, the cloud allows for collaboration on documents and is a central repository for documents that can be accessed through a variety of devices.

Among the growing number of options available for cloud service are Amazon (S3 Standard), Microsoft (OneDrive), Google (Google Cloud Storage), IBM (IBM Cloud), Dropbox (Dropbox Backup), Apple (iCloud), and BackBlaze (B2 Cloud Storage).

All offer apps with offline capabilities for Windows and macOS computers; and Android and iOS smartphones and tablets.

All are viable options. The key: Stay within your ecosystem as you consider cloud systems.

As Verizon 5G home managing partner Steven Sharp explains, "If you buy an iPhone, iPad, and MacBook, use iCloud as your primary backup. If you use an Android cell phone and Windows laptop, use Google Cloud as your primary backup. It helps you to build a seamless experience when you stay within the same ecosystem so the technology doesn't get in the way."

Payment options vary. A common method is to provide a limited amount of free storage — probably enough to suit your needs — and then charge bandwidth-usage fees on a pay-as-you-go basis for additional space and services. Apple's iCloud is built into every Apple device and users get the first 5 gig for free. BackBlaze offers the first 10 gig for free.

But annual cloud subscription fees, once your storage needs exceed the free capacity, never end. You have to be online to access it. Transfer speeds can be slow. And if you cancel your subscription, you will lose data and access to it.

Some experts warn also that the cloud can be hacked. But, according to Sharp, "The likelihood is small and it's probably because the user didn't set up secure parameters around their password."

Secure parameters include a strong alphanumeric password that includes symbols, characters, and numbers; and two-factor authentication (2FA). 2FA requires that same strong password and username and then an additional login credential to gain account access. Gaining that second credential requires access to information that belongs to you, such as your mother's maiden name or the street where you grew up.

External Hard Drive

External hard drives offer the advantage of local control. Unless someone breaks into your house and steals it, information on your external hard drive can't be hacked or stolen.

In addition, they are cheaper than ever. After you pay the one-time cost to purchase the device, you're done. You don't have recurring subscription and bandwidth-usage fees that are typical with cloud storage.

And their transfer speed is faster than the cloud.

You can pay more for an external hard drive that is compatible to both Microsoft and Macintosh if you live in both worlds.

But external hard drives become corrupted and die over time. You can't back them up remotely.

External hard drives come in two versions:

- HDD (Hard Disk Drive): an electromechanical device that uses movable read/write heads and spinning disks coated with magnetic material to store and retrieve digital data.
- SSD (Solid State Drive): uses integrated circuit assemblies as memory to store data in microchips. The SSD has been called an advanced version of the flash drive because it has no moving parts.

In general, SSDs can process and access data faster than HDDs, so if transfer speed is important to you SSDs are the way to go. They are typically more resistant to physical shock than HDDs and they run silently.

But they usually are more expensive than comparable HDDs and have less storage capacity.

If size is important, you may want an HDD. Larger SSDs are out there but so is their relative cost.

Most HDD's come with two- or three-year warranties but yours can last indefinitely, some experts say, if you keep it in one safe place and don't move it around.

If your storage needs are modest, one terabyte will be plenty and give you room for growth. If you want more, they're not that expensive; you can get up to 4TB for less than $100. When I wrote the first edition of this book, that price was $200.

Automatic backups can be scheduled to run at timed intervals; at a certain time of day; on a daily, weekly, or monthly basis; only if files have been updated or changed since a particular date; within a number of days; and other arranged times to suit your preference.

Which to Choose

Every backup option has its pros and cons. Decide which option you like the best and start using it immediately if you aren't already.

But, say most experts, use one or two of the runners up as well. While redundancy is the mark of a poorly edited manuscript, it is the sign of a strong backup system.

Remote Desktop Software

If you maintain both a laptop for mobile use and a desktop back at the office, check into a remote desktop application such as TeamViewer. Having this app running in both locations allows you to access any data on your office computer while sitting in a coffee shop halfway around the world working on your laptop.

This application is especially useful when you realize you accidentally left a document open on your office machine and forgot to save it. Rather than lose the progress you made on your laptop from having to merge the changes between the two, you can connect to the office machine, save the file, close it — and send it to yourself.

Appointment Book

I carry an appointment book with me everywhere. If you've made the leap to electronic appointment books, you're ahead of me. I'm happy with print. Just have a way to record your appointments so you can organize your life, meet your deadlines, and keep your focus on your writing.

Paper Clips

If you're totally e-based, you may have never used a paper clip. For me, because I still regularly use or receive paper, they are indispensable. I clip paper clips to the front cover of my appointment book. You can't do that with an electronic appointment book — but you probably don't need to.

Cell Phone and Charger

I resisted getting my first cell phone, thinking that it was just for making phone calls, and that being out of contact with the world gave me some kind of privacy. Now that I've got one, I can't live without it. Your cell phone and charger are important tools in your writer's kit.

You might also want to invest in a small external battery pack, in case you aren't going to be near a power outlet anytime soon and your internal battery is getting close to empty. You can get a small lightweight one that will charge your phone a couple of times for about $20.

Beverages

I always have a glass of iced tea or coffee at my table. What liquid drink works for you? Keep liquid flowing with as little sugar as possible.

But be careful around the laptop. One spill across the keyboard and you're out of business.

Mobile Office Carrier

I've got a strong knapsack for carrying around my portable office and for keeping the component parts always together so that I can relocate at a moment's notice. When it's full, it weighs about ten pounds. I used to sling it over my right shoulder. Now I strap in on both shoulders to distribute the weight evenly.

Either way, carrying around my knapsack becomes an isotonic exercise that forces me to walk with good posture, throw my shoulders back, and tighten my stomach muscles. It also helps me to breathe slowly and deeply.

If carrying around a knapsack doesn't fit your image or lifestyle, find the carrier that does. Just make sure it's durable, as light as possible, and you can fit your mobile office in it.

Bonus Items

Those items are your essentials but do whatever else you need to do to make your space comfortable. You'll be spending a lot of time there (see "What Is Your Writer's Space?").

- When you're at home, you control the music; at restaurants, you go with theirs. Or you can listen to your favorite music service quietly on your laptop.

- Pictures of loved ones? Whether in your wallet or purse, or on your cell phone or favorite social media sites, you've probably already got plenty of them.
- Affirmations? If they help, sure. Suggestion: Come up with your own.

Chapter 2

WHAT IS YOUR WRITER'S SPACE?

My supervisor at a college where I once taught said to me one day as I was freewriting in my journal, "Ah, the life of a writer. Sitting along the bank of a river, leaning against a tree, feeling the breeze in his hair as he writes."

Well, maybe that was his ideal writer's space. (I was actually sitting at my desk in a cramped office at the time.) It's not mine, as idyllic as it sounds.

Do you have a writer's space? As an author beginning a book, you've already committed yourself to completing a long journey through your mind. Where is that one physical place, or what are those numerous places, where you can return to day after day to concentrate on your writing and researching?

Do you prefer absolute silence when you work? At home, find a corner of a room at a quiet time of day or night or an empty room with a door. On the road, try a library. Many of them have glass-enclosed rooms where you can plug in your laptop and work peacefully.

Or do you prefer the buzz of activity in the background to stimulate your senses and keep you alert? Try a restaurant, or a coffee shop for writers, or a dining area inside a bookstore.

Find other places in your community where writers hang out and hang out there.

At home, play your favorite music in the background to set your mood and rhythm.

Ken Wachsberger

The Restaurant Attraction

As long as I've been writing and editing for publication, restaurants have been my primary office. Sometimes it was a restaurant where a friend worked. At others the attraction was the food.

But more often than not, it had a booth where I could spread out my books and papers, the wait staff and management welcomed me no matter how long I stayed or how little I spent, and they kept my coffee cup or iced tea glass full. After I purchased my first laptop, an electric outlet became necessary. Anything else — air conditioning, good music, herbal iced tea, a booth by the window, real cream instead of *ersatz*, cleanliness — was a bonus.

In years past, my favorite restaurants have belonged to chains. The conformity of branches around the country makes me feel at home wherever I travel. My current favorite is a Panera two miles from my home. It's clean. My table is all the way in the back so I never know what the weather has been until I leave at the end of my day.

But it's got an electric outlet on the wall next to it and it's located by the iced tea and the restroom. Music is an eclectic blend of songs and genres from the fifties through the eighties, and staff members welcome me as family no matter what time I arrive.

My presence for extended periods of time doesn't reduce wait staff tips because Panera doesn't have wait staff.

If the restaurant fills up during rush hour, I separate the two tables where I'm sitting and consolidate my books and papers onto the one with my laptop so a stranger can sit at the table next to me.

I sometimes buy food even when I'm not hungry just to say thanks.

Rent Asunder by My Accountant

For years, I saved all of my restaurant receipts and then at tax time told my accountant they were business expenses that I made because the restaurant was like my office, which made my food purchases the equivalent of rent for office space.

He said, "You're just eating a meal, like everyone else."

I countered, "But I only ate to preserve my space; I wouldn't have eaten otherwise."

But he didn't buy it. He said the owner would have to give me a rent receipt for me to call it rent, and then the owner would have to record my payments as rental income. And that was that.

Now I have to, well, eat the bill.

What's your writer's space?

Chapter 3

MAKE THOSE PRECIOUS MOMENTS COUNT

You have time, even in the busiest of weeks, to work on your book. If you want to be more productive as a writer despite a hectic daily work schedule, become familiar with your body clock. Go with your flow, not against it.

Figure out what hours are left after your workday is finished. If you work a day job, your remaining hours are in the early morning, late afternoon-early evening, and late night. Those are your choices. Which work better for you?

If you aren't sure, try them all and see which best fits your flow:

- Get up two hours early every morning, stop at a coffee shop on your way to work, and work on your book then.
- Or, stop in at the library on your way home after work and spend two hours there before completing your journey.
- Or, stay up two hours after your preferred bedtime and spend that time with your book.

If you can't spare two hours, write for one. One isn't two, but it's not zero either. It all counts.

Record your word output at all times. With Microsoft Word, the word count for your document appears at the bottom left side of the screen. When are you most productive? Once you start counting your words, you can give yourself realistic goals.

Ken Wachsberger

Working for Someone Else

When you work for someone else, you have to keep their hours even when your body clock is screaming otherwise.

Inspiration that hits in the middle of a company meeting cannot be developed. But you can jot down notes to develop later if you always have a spiral notebook with you even when you're away from your computer.

While you're at your day-job computer, keep a file open but minimized on the screen.

When a thought hits you, jot down whatever portion of it you can in however much time you can snatch to satisfy your own needs on company time. Most likely, by periodically emptying your mind even while at work, your productivity and focus on the job will increase because you will be less distracted by thoughts you are trying to remember for your book.

Or write during lunch.

Yes, we of the work force learn that lunch time is networking time, and it can be. But your network will understand if you tell them that you're working on deadline — the one that you set for yourself. They'll even give you encouragement, watch the progress of your book along the way, and be the first to buy your book when it comes out.

Working for Yourself

Working for yourself, you hopefully have more freedom to schedule flexibility.

Those flows that hit you in the middle of the day, with no other boss but yourself looking over your shoulder? Run with them.

Maximize the screen whenever you want and write until you're done.

You've Got the Time

No Matter Who Pays Your Bills

No matter how you are employed, you will have a weekend, though the days will vary from job to job and they may or may not be consecutive. Reserve some portion of that time to write.

As progress picks up on your book and writing frenzy kicks in, your family and loved ones will get progressively fewer hours with you — but when you're with them, you'll be fully with them, not secretly spacing out on your book (see "The Me-You-Us Theory").

Strive to Do Better Than the Minimum

As a book coach in my early days, I was too nice. I didn't want my clients to feel like failures so I allowed them to feel victorious if they wrote three times a week even for just a few minutes a day. Yes, that's better than nothing.

But strive to do better than the minimum. If you're a writer, writing is your job. You show up for work whether you feel like it or not. You produce something every day. As Stephen King said, "Amateurs sit and wait for inspiration; the rest of us just get up and go to work."

Write everyday no matter how much or how little you write each day. Those bursts of free moments that you discover when you aren't even looking are gifts, stray blocks of five minutes here and fifteen minutes there that regular people consider unworthy of being utilized wisely but writers recognize as indispensable:

- When you keep a notebook or recorder by the side of your bed to capture the flashes of brilliance that come to you in the middle of the night, you are a writer.
- When you carry a notebook in your back pocket or purse at all times, because there is never a time when memorable thoughts might not enter your mind and you want to be ready to capture them, you are a writer.

- When you keep your notebook on the front seat next to you while you're driving so that, when the perfect description to that scene you've been conceptualizing suddenly appears in your mind as brightly as the sun on the other side of the windshield, and you hang onto it until you get to the next stop sign or red light, then jot down a few words and phrases to expand later, you are a writer.

These hidden nuggets of time add up. You always have revising to do. Print out a weak chapter and carry it with you everywhere:

- Doctors' waiting rooms (Do you really need to read their magazines from the last decade?)
- Kids' after-school activities (Are those small-talk discussions with the other parents really that compelling?)
- In line at the grocer (No, wait; you've got to find out the latest Hollywood gossip)
- On the bus (Make progress while being transported from here to there)
- During commercials in front of the TV (or anywhere else you sit that gives you inspiration)

What are your favorite free-moment bursts?

And give yourself credit for the time you write. Don't sabotage your own efforts by saying, "I didn't do anything today? I just edited."

Quantity is less important than consistency. If you think you can't write one particular day, at least have a printout of what you're already written so you can read it at unplanned surprise opportunities. You'll naturally edit and revise — can you even help it? — and that counts.

Life Happens

But don't get too hung up on the time when you write. It's great if you can set aside a fixed amount of time every day at the same time but life happens. If another obligation sabotages your sacred time one day, don't write off the day. Just write at another time.

You've Got the Time

Some writers say they like to end the day in the middle of a thought so that the next time they sit down to write they can start there. That's not my style. I write and rewrite and reread until I've got nothing left to say or my schedule catches up with me and I have to shut down for the day. The next day, I regain my flow by reading and rereading what I wrote the previous day, or some other passage that needs improving, or some passage that is so good I wish I had written it and then realize that I wrote it. Self-hypnosis works.

Sleep is overrated, at least short term. An hour of motivation is worth two hours of sleep. When you're producing, your energy goes up even as your sleep hours go down. And you can catch up on your missing sleep hours during your weekend, whatever days that is for you.

It's true. Most of us don't have eight hours a day every day to write. We have to carve out precious moments throughout always hectic days and make them count.

You can do it, and increase your writing productivity, when you discover your body clock and go with your flow.

Chapter 4

NAME YOUR FILES SO YOU CAN FIND THEM

Create an electronic folder for your book as soon as you can and then allow your subfolders to form naturally. Don't let your files reside loosely on your desktop or in your primary folder. Otherwise, as the number of files pertaining to your book grows — and it will — they'll get out of hand and you won't be able to find the files you need when you need them.

Your files won't all be for sections of your manuscript, although that's what I'll be focusing on in this brief chapter. They may include text that you are writing for the website that will promote your book when it comes out, drafts of correspondence with typesetters, artists, printers, web developers, editors, groups that want to hire you as a speaker, and experts and celebrities who you are inviting to write forewords and testimonial quotes.

You'll create other files for your daily freewrites, head trips and journal entries, questions you need to answer, and experts to answer them.

All of them need to be carefully named so that at any time you can know what's in a file just by glancing at the filename and you can find the right file when you need to refer to it no matter how complex your folder system becomes.

How to Name Book Files

Here's how I name files for my books.

Begin with a brief phrase that describes the contents of the file. For your book, that phrase might be the title or a shortened version of it. Let multiple words in a phrase run together, with first letters capitalized for easy reading. An underscore ("_") completes the first phrase:

MyBookTitle_

While you are working on early drafts, consider creating a separate file for each chapter. When you're working on chapter 6, for example, it's a lot easier to print out the file for chapter 6 than to have to locate the pages that correspond to chapter 6 in your manuscript and print out only those pages. And you don't want to print out the complete manuscript to work on one chapter.

Here's how my filename would look:

MyBookTitle_chapter06_

Why do you want to print out any pages at all when you can work totally online?

So you can take advantage of those otherwise-wasted time periods that I wrote about in "Make Those Precious Moments Count." You can't always have your computer with you, and please don't think you can do your best editing off a cell phone. In addition, seeing your words on paper instead of on the screen gives you a different perspective on your writing. Errors in mechanics, grammar, and spelling that you missed on the screen jump out at you in print.

When you create separate files for the chapters in your book, you want them to line up in chronological order. You also don't want files that aren't parts of the manuscript — correspondence pertaining to your book, for instance — to fall in between successive chapters.

So, use the same pattern to name subsequent chapters, beginning with your descriptive prefix to the filename. Then include, as you saw from the example above, a variation of _chapter01_ in successive chapter filenames:

MyBookTitle_chapter01_
MyBookTitle_chapter02_

Dating Your Files

Next, date each file when you open it so you know at a glance how current the file is. Dating is another way to line up folders in chronological order but it has to be done carefully. For instance, you can't name them beginning with _January_ and ending with _December_ because the alphabetical order of the months isn't chronological.

But even using numerals, be careful. When you use six numerals, if you put the numerical elements in the order you speak them — "February 16, 2024" becomes "021624," for instance — you'll make it through the first year with the chronological order unscathed. But as soon as January of the following year comes around, it will jump in line ahead of February's files from the preceding year.

A better way to date files is to write the year first and then the month and date as you generally speak them, using eight digits: "February 16, 2024" becomes "2024 February 16" becomes "20240216."

Now, indicate what draft each file represents: _01, _02.

So, the filenames for the first drafts of your opening chapters will look like this:

    MyBookTitle_chapter01_20240216_01
    MyBookTltle_chapter02_20240216_01

When you begin working on the second draft of chapter 1, your chapters will line up like this:

    MyBookTitle_chapter01_20240216_01
    MyBookTitle_chapter01_20240216_02
    MyBookTltle_chapter02_20240216_01

I used to advocate changing the date for every draft but I've never actually found that practice to be useful unless I'm returning to the manuscript after a long time away from it. More important is to get the draft right. This phrase in your filename is hugely important when you're sharing files with someone else, for instance, your editor.

If you want to use Track Changes while you edit and then create a clean version to read for the flow, you can name the Track Changes file

MyBookTitle_chapter01_20240216_01_TrackChanges

and then rename the final draft

MyBookTitle_chapter01_20240216_01_Clean

Are you old enough to remember when WordPerfect allowed filenames to have only eight characters?

Creating the Manuscript File

When you compile all the individual chapters into one manuscript for the first time, give the filename some variation of

CompleteText_20240914_01

Draft two then is

CompleteText_20241123_02

Usually, you don't need information from previous drafts but often you do. Don't ask me to name instances. There are way too many.

Bonus Tip

Remember those people I noted at the top of this chapter who will likely be in regular communication with you throughout the writing of your book? Start a Word file for each one. In it, you summarize your Zoom calls. You reproduce all email messages. Jot down your random ideas as they relate to that person.

Naming files for people is easy: FirstLast_20240216_01

* * *

Have you ever misplaced a file and been unable to find it when you needed it? Get in the habit now of naming your files so they can be found quickly and easily, including early drafts.

PART 2: WRITING YOUR BOOK

Chapter 5

FREEWRITING: CREATING ORDER OUT OF CHAOS

Writing and publishing a book is an exhilarating, educational adventure. It will transform your life no matter the topic of your book or why you wrote it.

But when you're just starting out, the endeavor can appear intimidating. You may find yourself obsessing over the apparent confusion and overlook the actual simplicity.

Writing Isn't a Linear Process

The challenge is, writing isn't a linear process. You don't always do first this and then that and then the next thing. Chapter 1 isn't always the first chapter you write. Ideas can be developed in many possible orders.

How many thoughts do you have at any moment? Imagine all those thoughts as ideas that belong somewhere in your book and all have to be expanded.

Quick: Where does each idea go in your book? In what order? How do you tie them together?

You have no idea at that moment but if you spend too much time trying to figure it out in your head so you know what to write first, you'll forget every one of those thoughts, except maybe the one that got your attention first.

What happened to the other thoughts? Oh, they're still somewhere out there, or in there — in your brain. But you can't remember them anymore because they've already been replaced by new thoughts.

That's what happens when you have a brain. It thinks. Those early thoughts may return and you can write them down then. But they may not. They become cutting-edge thoughts lost forever because you didn't spit them out at the moment that you were having them, to organize and expand later.

An Outline Would Be Nice

It's true, the sooner you can crank out an outline, and then a table of contents, the faster you'll be able to write your book. For your high school term paper, what was your first assignment? "Tomorrow, bring me your five-part outline." Fifty years later, I can say that coming up with a table of contents is still a good idea.

And, in fact, to make your job easier, we do have several common outline options that find their way into most books, either individually or in combination, including

- **Chronological:** In writing your autobiography or telling a story, you can do what Elton John did in *Rocket Man*, his life story movie, and go back and forth between time periods and levels of consciousness. But most life stories and novels are chronological: First this happened, then this, and then this. Transition terms may include "later," "the next day," and "in the meantime."

- **Instructional:** This option usually follows one of two forms: how to do something yourself and how something was done. The first is written in second person polite command: First do this, then this, then this. A cake recipe or instructions on how to change a tire fall into this structure. The second tells a story in a way that is enlightening but probably doesn't enable you to duplicate it, such as, how the United States landed a man on the moon. This second form is similar to chronological. Transition terms are the same but they more likely will include "Finally."

- **Categorical:** Every election season candidates come out with books that spell out their campaign platforms. The rough outline is issue by issue: the current situation, how it got to be that way, the candidate's plan to fix it or make it better. Or, how can your readers develop self-esteem despite coming from abusive or broken homes? Discuss one category of suggestions at a time. Then offer a broad conclusion.

- **Cause-Effect:** A happened; as a result, B happened. The world far exceeded its wise use of fossil fuel; as a result, global warming is ravaging all parts of the world. You were teased as a child; as a result, you learned to use humor to fit in. This option ends with a series of suggestions to change negative behavior or make the best of positive behavior. Often it includes a call to action as well. I noted above how the options are often used in combination. *Rocket Man* fits this scenario. Why did the movie focus so heavily on his abusive parents? To explain in part how he became addicted to drugs.

- **Evaluative:** Should we get off fossil fuel entirely in favor of alternative fuels? The answer has passionate supporters on both sides and more in the middle supporting a combination of the two. What are your view's pros and cons? Using the evaluative structure, explain the significance of the overall issue and then weigh the pros and cons. Spell out your overall conclusion at the end.

- **Comparison-Contrast:** "When I was a kid back in the sixties...." Get ready for a comparison-contrast story about how life was better and also worse back when than it is now. In writing your book, take one category at a time: the music, the politics, the lifestyle, the clothing. Then describe it during both the sixties and now. You can draw individual conclusions after each topic and then one broad conclusion at the end.

If you can identify your book with one or more of these options, you already have an emerging vision of your final outline.

But don't get hung up on an outline or table of contents if you don't have it yet; writers have written complete books without them. Focus instead on writing and the outline will emerge, and then the table of contents, whether you're writing fiction, nonfiction, self-help, academic, or any other kind of book. If the outline doesn't emerge right away, if it isn't obvious to you at first, don't go comatose.

Start freewriting. Actors have a mantra for times of stress: "When in doubt, slow down." Writers have another for when your flow is obstructed: "When in doubt, freewrite."

Use notepad, desk notebook, journal, laptop computer, napkin, or whatever tool you have on hand to start making notes but get to your computer as soon as you can because that's where writers develop and clean up manuscripts.

During freewriting, you write whatever you want with no regard to topic, order, or coherency with full faith that it will all come together in the end.

You've already got thoughts developing in your mind. Are you imagining chapter titles, thinking of who you need to interview, flashing on stories that illustrate main points that you'll want to include somewhere, wondering who would want to read your book anyway? Get them out. Scatter your deepest, your craziest, your funniest, your most desperate and heroic of thoughts and ideas across the pages like air from a burst balloon.

We're writers, not rememberers.

It's a Messy Process

All those crazy thoughts you've been holding in: "I'm no good. I'm not smart. I don't have time. I'll never find a publisher." If you have those thoughts swirling around in your head, they're taking up valuable real estate that your good ideas need to grow.

So, get them out of your head and onto your paper or screen even if you know you will throw many of them out later. Spit them out, throw them out, and keep freewriting.

And something interesting is going to happen along the way. You're going to start thinking more about your book and less about those fears. Before you know it, the crazy ideas will dissipate and the good ideas will predominate.

You've Got the Time

Why? That's just how the brain works. Accept it as a gift from the universe and don't dwell on it unless your book is about how the brain works.

It's a messy process. But during freewriting, go wild. Ignore errors in mechanics, grammar, and spelling. You'll get to them later. Fragments, comma splices, and run-on sentences are fine for now. Express ideas using only simple subject-predicate sentences if you want. Use "thing" when you can't think of the right noun; and "very" when you can't think of the right modifier. Write notes to yourself in the middle of the text using **[bold square brackets]** so they stand out from the main text.

Mental Blocks and Timeouts

If you get a mental block while you're freewriting, think about these questions:

- What is my book about?
- Why do I want to write it?
- Why am I qualified to write it?
- What makes it unique in its field?
- Who is my audience?
- Where am I now in the book-writing process?
- How much time am I willing to put into it?
- How urgent am I to finish it?

Freewrite about these ideas. A thought doesn't have to end up in the book to be considered valuable in helping you to write the book — and you can turn it into a blog entry at a later date.

Or take a break and walk away from your laptop.

- Stretch.
- Have a light snack.
- Take a walk.
- Watch a half hour of TV.
- Make phone calls.
- Catch up on your email and social media.

- Fold laundry.
- Meditate.

But always keep your notebook with you because as soon as you walk away from your laptop and allow your mind to relax, it will start producing new thoughts and ideas. No, not all the time. Sometimes your mind is just burnt out from thinking creatively and needs a rest.

Other times, as soon as you walk away from the strict focus and allow your mind to relax, blocked thoughts that were hiding behind the stress will emerge. Be ready to capture them. You can type them when you get back to your laptop and move on from there.

Literary Chaos

In the early stages of your writing, one of your biggest challenges will be to overcome the inertia of inaction. Think Newton: An imagination at rest stays at rest until acted upon by an opposing force — a threatening competitor, a relentless coach, a cup of coffee….

Write for as long as you think you can. Then write for five minutes more. Don't make excuses for poor performances. Every performance is an accomplishment worthy of celebration. And you'll do better next time.

That's what Olympic champions tell themselves when they underperform. You're building endurance as you grow stronger as an Olympic writer. Your consciousness will expand. You'll achieve new heights in your field. And you'll realize that it's no different now than it was then: Sometimes you have productive days and sometimes you don't.

And what are you left with?

Literary chaos.

You've got ideas going in every direction, some complete and poetically arranged, others a cacophony of unordered phrases and questions repeated numerous times from different angles. Some don't have anything to do with your book: what you had for breakfast, phone calls you've got to make before the day is done, household chores you've been meaning to complete, ideas for other books and stories you're thinking of writing someday. The order is so chaotic, mortals fear it. But writers seek it out and confront it, and then they tame it. How do you do that?

The Miracle: Cut and Paste

First, if you didn't do your freewriting on your computer, type your notes into your computer at your first opportunity.

Next, embrace the miracle of the digital age for writers: Cut and Paste. If you're forty years old or younger, you probably grew up with Cut and Paste. Feel free to skip over this section if you want. If you're older than forty and you haven't typed since college, read on.

Cut and Paste are the functions on Microsoft Word that enable you to categorize your freewriting and organize it into a coherent order. It's so simple but their value is unlimited in helping you to group ideas, order groups, and order ideas within groups.

You can find the icons under the Home tab. Simply highlight the word or phrase that you want to move, hit Cut, and it disappears. Then move the cursor to where you want the text to appear and hit Paste.

Another way to move text is to highlight the text that you want to move, hold down the Ctrl key, and type either X to copy and delete the text or C to copy it but not delete it. Move the cursor to where you want the text to go, hold down Ctrl, and type V to paste it there. With Ctrl + X, your operation is accomplished. With Ctrl + C, you still have to go back to the original location and delete the text.

I prefer Ctrl + C, but there's no right or wrong way. Sometimes, I use Ctrl + C and then hit Delete so I don't have to return to that spot after I paste the text in its new location. Don't get hung up on which method is right. They all enable you to write with abandon in any order you choose with full confidence that you will be able to make sense out of it all or revert to what you had if you decide you don't like the changes you just made. Use them to create order out of chaos. Here's how:

Using Cut and Paste

You probably noticed as you were typing your freewrite that similar ideas repeated themselves.

With Cut and Paste, you can take an incomplete idea that appears on page 2 and move it to page 1 ahead of an incomplete idea on page 1 that is on the same subject. Related ideas may appear on other pages as well. Use Cut and Paste to bring them all together.

Group ideas belonging to other subjects in the same way. Consider straggler ideas as their own subjects. Your book takes a leap forward in progress and you feel a corresponding burst of relief when you find that you've categorized all of your thoughts to date and compiled them in a finite number of subjects.

Now scan the subjects. Which one looks like it would appear first? Highlight it. Then cut it from wherever it is in your notes file, move your cursor to the top of the page, and paste it.

What subject is next? Repeat the process but paste the text where text for the first subject ends. Repeat until all subjects are in their proper order. If some subjects defy order, leave them at the end of the file. They aren't ready yet to be ordered.

Creating Order out of Chaos

An order is emerging — not yet an outline but some sense, a flow.

Don't stop. Now that you've put the subjects in order, put the thoughts in order within the first subject to the best of your ability — if it's too early for order to be an issue, don't worry about it. You'll get there.

Repeat for the other subjects.

And those extraneous ideas about daily chores, other writing projects, and paralyzing head trips? They served a purpose during freewriting. They helped you to clear your mind and connect those scattered thoughts that actually pertained to your book. But their usefulness is done. Delete them or move them into their own files if you want to refer to them later.

Now read your notes, with your fingers on the keyboard, always ready to type. Read them again.

As you develop familiarity with the ideas, your mind naturally begins to fill in the details as it focuses on each thought one at a time. Your fingers want to type. Let them and watch your thoughts expand on the screen.

Those pearls of profundity that made perfect sense in your mind but need more than one sentence to make sense to others? Read them as if you were someone who doesn't know the inner workings of your mind and answer the questions that naturally arise or raise the questions yourself in **[bold square brackets]** to confront later.

Gaps in the text show up as you try to leap from the end of one thought to the beginning of the next and the words don't flow. You realize that transitional words must be added to connect the two thoughts. Or, they may be component parts of separate chapters. You don't know what they are yet or how many pages they will fill so you write **"[trans]**," which tells you to come back to that passage later. Then keep on going so you don't lose your flow.

Listen. You can hear your mind humming, "Here's a thought. Here's a thought. Here's a thought. Here's a thought."

Don't let them pass into oblivion. Type them.

Throughout this process, you've gone from freewriting to brainstorming to editing all while order is emerging. During freewriting, you write whatever you want. In brainstorming, you write whatever you want pertaining to your topic.

Brainstorming is freewriting with a focus. You may hear the terms being used interchangeably. Don't waste your time trying to parse connotations or determine when one ends and the other begins. You'll be doing plenty of both while you write your book. During editing, you look at what you've already written and make it better.

Out of chaos comes order. First create the chaos.

It all begins with freewriting.

Chapter 6

TURNING YOUR FREEWRITE INTO A BOOK

Give that freewriting file that you're about to open a name so you can find it later. If today is July 21, 2024, call it Freewrite_20240721_01 (see "Name Your Files So You Can Find Them"). When you freewrite tomorrow, you'll want to return to this file.

Build on Your Initial Freewrite

Later, when you freewrite again on a totally different part of the book or about an unrelated issue, name it Freewrite_, the day's eight-digit date, and _01 so that your freewrites line up together and in chronological order in your file folder.

Add new material to the bottom of your current file. Then use Cut and Paste to classify and sort your new ideas with the others. Many of them will be similar to the ideas from previous freewrites. Group them together, order the ideas so that they make sense, and eliminate redundancy. Other ideas will break new ground. Add them wherever you think they belong.

Now read the complete file from the beginning, with your fingers on the keyboard. Automatically your mind will want to expand. Liberate your fingertips so that they type whatever your mind is thinking as you think it. Self-hypnosis works.

You'll add key phrases and ideas that belong somewhere in the book, questions that you'll need to research, and clarifications of what you wrote the day before. You'll think of experts you'll want to interview. You'll put it all in order later.

When you can see that one set of ideas is the embryo of a particular chapter, copy it and paste it into its own file, where it will be easier to develop. Name it and future chapter files, as they come together, so that they all line up in manuscript order (see "Name Your Files So You Can Find Them"). When they are all finished, you'll bring them together into a complete manuscript file.

Writing Your Chapters

Look where you've come so far. From a blank sheet of paper, you've freewritten, brainstormed, edited, expanded, discovered the beginnings of your table of contents, and begun to create separate chapter files. Give each file a working chapter title. Write it at the top of the page, centered, in bold. It will be the first words you see every time you open that file.

You're way past your initial freewriting at this point.

Now open up one file. Pick any one. It doesn't matter where you begin. It may be where you have the "low-hanging fruit." In other words, you know a lot about that chapter already and won't need to do a lot of research to complete it. You can write major portions off the top of your head.

Or maybe you like to begin with a challenge. Start with the chapter you know already will be the hardest to complete.

Now read it and reread it with your fingers on the keyboard. Those brief notes that you wrote in two or three sentences yesterday are now calling out to be expanded. Focus on one of them and write as much as you can while you've got your flow, disregarding all conventions concerning mechanics, grammar, and spelling for now.

What questions come up that you will need to answer? Type them when they arise. What research do you need to do? Who do you need to interview? What other ideas come to mind that belong in the chapter? What sources do you need to consult? What keywords will help you find answers to your questions?

If an idea comes up that belongs in a different chapter of your book, type it now but make a notation to move it to the appropriate file later.

Get Rid of Junk Thoughts

Those ideas for your to-do list of personal and business chores? Type them up, too. You'll transfer them to your appointment book later.

Adding those non-book thoughts to your writing doesn't diminish your flow because you've got an overall focus now: the title of that chapter. In fact, writing those extraneous thoughts helps you keep focused because by writing them down they no longer clutter your mind and you don't have to worry about forgetting them when you need them.

The process of freewriting and brainstorming is always available for you throughout the writing of your book. According to the respective definitions, you're now brainstorming. Don't get lost wondering which you're doing at any given moment.

This is the time to read, and reread, and re-reread. Print out a chapter-in-progress and glance at it in free moments, while you're waiting for your lunch to arrive at the restaurant, while you're in line at the supermarket, during commercials in front of the TV before bedtime.

Read it out loud when you can and feel the rhythm of your words. Where does it flow? Where does it feel awkward?

Expand by Anticipating

In many cases, you know the complete thought or the complete description. It's clear in your mind. Have you expressed it fully on paper? Your readers can't read your mind. Read what you've already written, but as if you were someone else. Does it raise questions? In many cases, if the text raises a question, that's the spot where the answer goes.

For instance, you wrote: "A fire broke out at a house on Main Street." What questions arise? One, for instance, is "When?" You know the answer. You were there in fact watching the fire fighters put it out. But your readers don't know. They're counting on you to tell them.

Anticipate the questions your readers will have and answer them in the text, often immediately. If you don't know an answer and you have to do the research to find out but you're experiencing a flow, write the question in **[bold square brackets]** so that it jumps out at you every time you read it. Then keep writing.

When the Flow Stops

But when the flow stops, it's time to do the research. Research is so simple with the Internet. Have it at your disposal for quick checks. While you can't count on it for all your answers, it will answer many of them and often can suggest places to go for more answers.

Do a search in your document for "[" (left square bracket) to easily find all your in-text queries.

Another major source of information comes from personal interviews. Seek out experts who will give you in-depth answers that you can record as direct quotes or paraphrases if you ask good open-ended questions (see "Conducting Interviews").

Your goal is to eliminate all the square brackets by finding answers to all your questions, and then tighten the text so it expresses your clearest thoughts with the fewest words. Know the reading level of your desired audience and choose words appropriately.

Use Subheadings

Break up long chapters by using subheadings.

You're writing to communicate and subheadings make it easier for readers to follow. But be consistent throughout your book even if you allow exceptions. For instance, chapters of five hundred words or less may not require subheadings but longer chapters will.

What you don't want is a 1,200-word chapter having subheadings and one of the same length or shorter not having subheadings.

You've Got the Time

Lean in the direction of having subheadings. They bring order to your text, they keep your readers' attention focused, they enable your readers to skim, and they give visual relief to content-heavy text.

Use Short Paragraphs

When you're writing articles for the Internet, we're told by Internet experts, stick with 1- and 2-sentence paragraphs and use a lot of bullets. You don't have to go to that extreme with your book. On average, paragraphs should have no more than four to six sentences.

Academics are notorious for using paragraphs that seem to go on forever. They may be shocked to learn that the perceived level of your writing expertise does not increase with the length of your paragraphs. Give your readers a break. They need white space to ease eye strain and increase comprehension.

- Search for topic sentences buried within long paragraphs and use them to begin new paragraphs.
- With dialogue, let each new speaker begin a new paragraph.

Writing the Conclusion and Introduction

When you've completed the final chapter, it's time to write the conclusion, which is the part of the book that wraps it all up, answers final questions, and delivers your parting message.

And then you write your introduction. No, not always. You're urged to write it last because the introduction gives you an overview of what your readers can expect from your book; and before you write it you probably don't completely know.

But if you know from the start the main ideas that you will be expressing throughout your manuscript and feel fully capable of writing your introduction immediately or at least beginning it, do it. But consider it a draft and read it again when the rest of your book is finished in case you want to tweak it.

Creating Your Manuscript

Congratulations. All your chapters are done. Your introduction and conclusion are done.

Now put them all together into one file and name it so you can find it when you need it (see "Name Your Files So You Can Find Them").

Chapter 7

TITLING AND SUBTITLING YOUR BOOK

Start thinking of a title as soon as you start conceptualizing the book. If you're writing a nonfiction book, it should have two parts: the main title and the subtitle. The title is a catchy phrase that relates to the theme of the book and will attract your readers. The subtitle explains what the title means.

Often the subtitle will be your working title while you're writing the book before you've come up with the right catchy phrase. Then suddenly the catchy phrase jumps out at you.

For example, I wrote a World War II book about Bernard Mednicki, a Belgian Jew who fled the country with his wife and children when the Nazis invaded, moved to southern France, posed as a Christian, and, through a series of incidents, found himself in the Maquis, the French resistance.

I was so fascinated with the idea of a Jew in the Maquis that the subtitle immediately presented itself: *A Jew in the Maquis*. Only at the end of the story, where Bernard lands on Ellis Island with his family, recalls the experience they have just survived, and says, "Never be afraid," did I know that the complete title of his story would be *Never Be Afraid: A Jew in the Maquis*. In my second edition of the book, I resubtitled it *A Belgian Jew in the French Resistance* to attract potential readers who might not know what the Maquis was.

Other titles are obvious right from the start. For the second of my two Holocaust books, I helped a child survivor of the concentration camp Auschwitz and her American-born husband to write her autobiography. When they presented the project to me, the title was *A Young Child's Journey through the Holocaust*, a reasonable title that, I thought, explained roughly what the story was about but didn't differentiate it from what my agent referred to as "a glut of Holocaust literature."

But what fascinated me about her story was that she had been in the last selection of the entire war. Anyone who knows Holocaust history knows of the infamous Dr. Mengele, the Angel of Death, who would line up the inmates of Auschwitz and then point to them one at a time and say, "You to the right" or "You to the left."

If you were selected to go to the left, you knew you were about to be cremated. Thirteen-year-old Golda was selected along with a hundred women, including her mother.

But unlike every selection that had come before hers, the Nazis didn't carry that one out. The Soviets were getting close to the border of Auschwitz, so the Nazis had to start their cover-up. The women were released.

Some forty years later, Golda now was probably the only person still alive who had survived the last selection of the war. The complete title was obvious to me: *The Last Selection: A Child's Journey through the Holocaust.* (We decided "Young Child" was redundant.)

Other titles serve the purpose of highlighting a main argument. This book is a good example. As a book coach, "I don't have time" is the number one excuse I hear from writers and others for why they "can't" start writing their books. Yes, you do have the time, if you have the desire.

So, I confronted their excuse head on by titling my book *You've Got the Time.* Call it a catchy phrase but, alas, 1. I'm not the only author who has chosen that exact title; and 2. Time for what? My subtitle is unique and answers that primary question: *How to Write and Publish That Book in You.*

Chapter 8

CONDUCTING INTERVIEWS

As an author of both fiction and nonfiction books, I'll never be the one to disparage their research value.

But books, because they take so long to go from conception to publication, are largely dated by the time they are available for purchase.

Articles in newspapers, magazines, and blogs, while informative and interesting — and more current than books — seldom address the immediate nuances of your concerns.

There is no better way to find out what developments occurred yesterday in your field of research or what solutions might be applied to your specific concerns than to interview an expert who is involved in the field.

Preparing for the Interview

In order to be successful in your interview, you need to prepare properly for it. Like painting a room, your ultimate success comes from paying attention to the details ahead of time.

The following three steps constitute the Dos and Don'ts for setting up and preparing for your personal interview:

1. Do set up your interview in advance.

In other words, don't expect your expert to be waiting to greet you when you show up for an unannounced hour interview. Likewise, don't just send an attachment of twenty questions in an email message and expect twenty in-depth answers.

You have two main ways to set up your interview properly, each with its own benefits and disadvantages.

Email

Email is one easy way if you have an email address. Be personable and friendly. Show passion. Be respectful.

Say who you are, explain what you want, and ask for a reply by a specific deadline.

Here's a model you can try for the body of your introductory letter. In well-developed paragraphs, say:

- Who you are
- Why you desire this person's expertise and by when
- How long it will take
- Range of desired dates
- Specific date by which time you need a response
- How and when you can be best reached and give phone number and email address
- Thanks in advance for getting back to you as soon as possible

Remember to edit your letter carefully before you send it. Don't blow this opportunity to show off your writing skills.

Telephone

If you have the phone number, the telephone works wonders. Even "important" people generally are reachable either at home or at work. Phone numbers are everywhere on the Internet. Get over the mystique and make the call.

But don't be surprised if the person you're calling isn't the person who picks up the phone, especially if you're calling the office. That's what receptionists are for: to run interference, to screen calls so that only the most important reach their target. Or the most courteous. Please don't forget the role of courtesy. Be someone the receptionist would like to be interviewed by.

However, don't count on being patched through on your first attempt. It's amazing but somehow important people always are "in a meeting" or "just stepped out." I think receptionists learn in orientation to never patch through unexpected callers on the first attempt. In any case, on your first call, prepare for rejection and follow-up.

Explain your purpose.

Briefly explain the topic of your book and why you would like an interview. In this way, your desired expert can weigh the pros and cons of talking about that subject with a total stranger for no pay and only some ego stroking that comes from being recognized as an expert.

> **Hint:** If you get nervous on the phone and you're scared that you'll screw up and go groupie in front of the expert, write your opening script. Then practice saying it out loud until it sounds like you're talking off the top of your head.

But, assuming the positive — because how many of us don't like to be recognized as experts in our own time? — it also allows time for your expert to prepare for the interview, to psych up for it, and, as often happens, to gather supplemental material to give you — for example, an article that just appeared in a trade journal that the office subscribes to but that you never heard of, that isn't available electronically, and that your library doesn't own.

Ask for the time you need.

If you are requesting an in-person interview, generally ask for no more than an hour. Then plan to stick to it. If you need some more time at the end of the hour, you can ask for it then. If you have established rapport during the interview, you'll probably get it right away or be invited back for a second session. Before hanging up, I always leave my phone number and email address with the receptionist and ask for my expert to call or email me back. I'm an optimist; I always hope for a miracle.

But I also ask for my expert's email address or, if I'm refused, for the receptionist's email address if she would be so kind as to forward my detailed request. In either case, here is your chance to shine literarily. Write from the heart. Say who you are, what your book is about, the broader topic of your questions, and why it is this person whose answers you want. Don't send your questions yet unless you have just one or two. Here, you're still seeking permission to send them.

With good fortune and the most brilliantly written of requests, you may get an answer within two weeks. But don't hold your breath waiting for it. The next caller likely will be you again. So, at the end of that first phone call, do not be a stranger. In saying goodbye, I always have some variation on the following exchange:

"By the way, what is your name?"

"Leslie."

"Well, thanks a lot, Leslie. I appreciate your help."

Ostensibly, I'm asking for the receptionist's name to say goodbye. But in fact, at the same time, I'm writing in my notes: "Receptionist — Leslie." The next time I call, when the receptionist picks up the phone, I say, "Hi Leslie, this is Ken Wachsberger." I've moved the discussion onto a first name basis.

2. Do your homework before your interview.

This step assumes an eventual yes answer. Congratulations. Now what? If the person you're interviewing belongs to an organization that is pertinent to your book, read literature on the organization. If you know of articles the person has written on your subject, read them. Let your questions rise to the level of your expert's expertise.

A personal example: I was invited by a progressive Jewish publication, *Present Tense*, to write an article on the Arabic community of Detroit, the largest Arabic community in the world outside the Middle East. I had no idea at the time but I did what I always do when I'm given an assignment. I said, "Sure, no problem." Then I panicked.

But I also began doing background research. I found a book on the Arabic community in America, which had an entire section devoted to the Arabic community of Detroit. I read it three times and took extensive notes.

I learned that the greater Detroit community was home to a mosaic of Arabic subcultures. Christian Palestinians lived here. Muslim Palestinians lived there. Maronites, Melkites, Chaldeans, Coptic Egyptians, and others lived in their own communities throughout the city and the surrounding suburbs. Some were largely blue-collar factory workers, others shopkeepers and professionals. The more I learned about the different communities, the more I realized I didn't know.

Then I called the co-editors, who, lo and behold, were totally reachable because they taught at colleges nearby where I lived. When I spoke to them on the phone, they could tell I was knowledgeable on the subject; I was sincere in my desire to write an authoritative, fair story; and I respected their expertise. The subsequent interview and the introductions they gave me to members of the different Arabic communities became the foundation of this article and a second one I wrote for a local newspaper.

3. Do prepare a list of well-written questions arranged in a logical sequence.

In other words, don't wing it and risk the chance of getting off on an unrelated tangent. The mind wants to work in a logical way. It seeks order. Help it out. Go with your mind's flow. The sequence of a well-organized list of questions actively suggests the outline of the interview write-up.

Begin with a freewrite.

List every question that comes to mind. Don't worry about wording of every question or even if your thought is a complete question. Write or type as fast as you can think — only you have to read your notes or understand your scribbles.

As a mental exercise, you might see how many questions you can list in ten minutes. Don't censor your thoughts: Is it a stupid question? Will he be able to answer it?

Now read them over and add some more. Think of the journalistic Five Ws and an H — Who? What? When? Where? Why? and How? — and fashion questions around them.

Notice that throughout this exercise you most likely have touched on related topics at different points in your freewrite. That's okay for a freewrite, but you can't ask the questions in that order because you will confuse your expert, who then won't be able to get their own flow in answering your questions.

Find related questions and group them together.

If you're writing about the person's life, you might group the questions by what period of life they cover: childhood, young adulthood, adulthood. Thank the Cut and Paste functions on your personal computer for making this step a joy (see "Freewriting: Creating Order out of Chaos").

Put the groups in their logical order.

Look at the groups of questions. Which would be the best group to begin your interview? In the example above, if you're writing the person's life story, you might want to arrange the groups chronologically — begin with the childhood questions, then the young adulthood questions, then the adulthood questions.

Put the questions in order within each group.

Now look at that first group of questions. I'll bet one of them is better than all the rest to open up the formal interview. Find it and label it number one. Which one comes next? Next? Use Cut and Paste to order the questions in group one; then move on to group two and so on until all the questions in all the groups are in a logical, flowing order.

Determine which questions, if any, should be answered before you go into the interview and answer them.

These might include questions about the group your interviewee belongs to that are answered in the group's own literature and website or are readily available over the Internet.

Eliminate all "Yes/No" questions and all "Either/Or" questions.

Why should you eliminate all "Yes/No" questions from your initial list? Because the answer is always "Yes" or "No." Boring. Interviews become good reading when you obtain colorful quotes from well-written, open-ended questions. Which question will give you better mileage: "Do you like your job?" or "What do you like and dislike most about your job?"

Same goes for "Either/Or" questions: "Ms. Voter, do you prefer the Democratic plan or the Republican plan?" or "What are the pros and cons of the Democratic and Republican plans?"

Keep it simple.

While you're at it, eliminate all complex, convoluted, multipart questions that confuse the person who's supposed to be helping you unravel your own confusion: "What is your opinion on…? What I mean by that is…? In other words,..?" Find one way to word the question and ditch the rest.

Don't forget your introductory questions.

In an in-person interview, the rapport-building stage begins with the initial handshake and the first few small-talk questions. The best ones emerge from your immediate observations. For instance, if you see a backpack in the corner of the room, you might say, "I see you're a hiker," and find yourself listening to an exciting story about a recent trek through the backwoods of Kentucky. In your enthusiasm, you'll think of your own questions on the spot. But if you feel the need to take out an insurance policy, think of a few good small-talk questions beforehand.

My friend, Pulitzer Prize-winning journalist Sheryl James, suggests one more question to begin your interview:

> The first thing I do once I sit down with someone to begin my interview is ask this question: "Do you have any questions for me?" Not only does this show respect, but I can't tell you how often the person I'm interviewing does in fact have a question. So many people have never been interviewed before, so it helps reduce stress also.

Congratulations! You've freewritten an in-depth list of questions; you've grouped them together and ordered the groups; you've ordered the questions within each group, eliminated all closed-ended "Yes/No" and "Either/Or" questions, tightened up any confusing questions, and even added a few introductory questions to break the ice.

You are ready to show your expert that you are an interviewer to be taken seriously. You have made it as easy as possible for them to answer all your questions clearly and provide you with good quotes along the way, and you have given yourself an outline that will enable you to write up your report easily afterwards.

Are you nervous? Of course, you are — because you're passionate about your book. That nervousness is your passion coming together with your creative energy. If you've followed the above three detailed steps, the interview itself will be easy.

A Few Pointers

A few pointers to keep in mind during the interview:

Courtesy Counts

Remember that courtesy counts. Dress nicely — not necessarily in your holiday best but not in dirty jeans either.

Address the person you're interviewing as Mr. or Ms. (or any special title, such as Dr. or Senator) unless told otherwise or you feel close enough to go straight to first person. That's got to be a judgment call. What you think is personable someone else might consider insulting. Err on the side of being too formal. As my friend, author and networking expert Greg Peters, says, "Better to be invited to friendship than slapped for impropriety."

Maintain good eye contact. Sit straight up. Lean forward. All you're doing here is showing that you're feeling alert and paying attention. If you don't pay attention, why should your expert?

Listen and Observe

Spend most of your time listening and observing. The writers' mantra is, "You have two ears and one mouth; spend twice as much time listening as talking." This isn't your time to sound brilliant. It's your time to seek brilliance. Ask one question at a time. Then wait for the answer.

While you're listening, you can observe your expert's surroundings, which may suggest more questions, as well as provide clues as to your expert's personality.

Be alert for good quotes.

Be flexible. Logically you will ask your questions in the order you typed them. But if you ask question number 3 and the answer also takes in questions 8, 9, and 10, you're not going to say, "Hey, hold on. I'm not there yet." Go with your interviewee's flow. You may even follow up the completed answer by asking question number 11 if it's part of the same group that included question 10. Check off your list all the questions that are being answered whether or not you ask them. At the next opportunity, you can return to question 4 and proceed.

Respect the silence. If you are a beginning writer, you may be tempted to interpret silence as your expert's boredom or lack of attention. But look above at steps 1 to 3 of the preparation stage. You've spent a lot of time preparing the best questions you could come up with. Now your expert needs time to formulate equally good answers.

Don't Argue

Don't argue, but do challenge. When you interview politicians, for instance, you can be confident that nearly every answer they give you is framed around political motives. You even may be certain at times that they're lying. But this isn't the time to show your political savvy because, if you personally attack someone's credibility, you can expect the interview to end right there.

So, don't use your words; use a political opponent's: "Senator Smith, you claim that your bill will preserve farmland while lowering taxes but your opponent has produced documentation that shows not only that taxes will go up but that farmland will decrease. How do you respond to those allegations?"

Expect the Best

Do expect the best possible answers to your questions.

- If you don't understand an answer, seek clarification: "I'm unclear what you mean by that. Could you please clarify?"
- If your question isn't answered completely, ask for more information: "How can you elaborate?"
- If the answer is a generalization, ask, "What specific details or examples illustrate this point?"
- If an answer raises another question, ask it on the spot. It's okay to not understand. If you knew all the answers, you'd be the one being interviewed.

And just because the question wasn't on your original list doesn't mean you shouldn't ask it. Put your list aside altogether and go with your flow if the opportunity arises.

Final Four Questions

At the end of the interview, ask these four informal questions:

1. Is there anything you would like to add?

You ask this question so your interviewee can clarify any answers he or she felt were less than adequate; and also because, despite all your preparation, you might have totally missed an important question or area of questions.

2. What other sources of information might help me in my search?

Remember, this is one of the reasons why you indicate your subject when you call to arrange for the interview, so your interviewee can gather books, articles, and any electronic sources that might be helpful to you.

3. Who else do you suggest I talk to?

Your interviewee knows other experts who can offer nuance and detail to your questions. Ask for referrals. Don't forget to ask for phone and email. If you've built trust during the interview, you can usually count on getting one or both if they are available.

4. May I call or email you if I have any follow-up questions?

Even though the answers to your questions all seemed to make sense while you were sitting in the interview, as soon as you get home and start organizing your notes, questions will arise. If you were scared to call the first time to set up the interview, you'll probably be more scared to call back and "sound stupid." This question anticipates the inevitable questions. If the answer is "yes," then don't give it a second thought when the time comes.

Email Interviews

For the intimate thrill of the experience, in-person interviews can't be beat. For simplicity and convenience on both ends, go for the email interview when you can. They're

- easier to set up;
- easier to conduct; and
- easier for interviewees to answer questions clearly and at their own convenience (though give a deadline by +when you need the answers).

And you don't need to transcribe them.

Likely you'll receive answers that are longer and more detailed than you need. They'll include typos, repetition, and extraneous anecdotes.

You can edit them. Get rid of puff. Delete redundancy. Shape the answer to fit your space.

But never alter the meaning; and respectfully share the revised quotes with your interviewee for approval.

Or ask in advance if it will be okay for you to edit for brevity and clarity. You can count on a grateful, "Please do."

Digital Recording

Another type of live interview can be done with digital recording. I encourage you to record as many interviews as you can:

- Digitizing your interview provides you with a permanent record that you can refer to later if you are working on an article or paper that covers the same material.

- It fills in those segments of information that you miss in your note taking.
- Especially if the subject matter is technical or contains many statistics, it is insurance that you don't, for instance, write 179 when you mean to write 197.
- If you're a beginner, listening to your interview later is an opportunity for you to critique your performance.

Digital recorders make it so easy to record an interview, including using your phone if you want, that you might be tempted to just put the pen and paper or laptop away.

Don't.

Although it's easy to get the words onto the recorder, it's a lot harder to get them off even with transcribing foot pedals that stop and start your interview; and even when you don't have to purchase an expensive transcriber because that same slow-down capability is in your digital recorder.

But it's easier than it used to be. My friend, Greg Peters, for example, used to do digital interviews using his cell phone and an app called TapeACall. But then along came Zoom:

> Since most of my meetings are on Zoom, that has proved to be pretty easy to use for recordings, both video and audio-only. In fact, I am in the process of developing a new online course on the fundamentals of good networking and will be using Zoom – its recording ability, and the fact that it can provide me with the transcript of the interview — as a part of my market research process.

Meanwhile, audio-to-text speech recognition systems keep improving. Traditionally they would pound out phonetic similarities to what was actually said in one long paragraph and then leave out the punctuation. Newer software yields more accurate transcripts and adds punctuation and formatting. It recognizes when speakers change. It can interpret low-quality recordings. You can add custom words to the app's vocabulary.

National Speaker Association member Ryan Morton relies heavily on voice-to-text to write his speeches. Transcribing services he uses mostly are tenmi.com, which charges ten cents a minute; and rev.com, which, Ryan says, "may be better with colloquialisms."

But won't a recorder, even a digital recorder, intimidate the person you're interviewing? Maybe forty years ago it would have but not in today's digital world. More likely, the person doing the interviewing is more intimidated.

Of course, you will need to ask permission beforehand — I usually ask when I arrive for the interview. If you receive it, then set up your recorder and settle in for a most amazing hour of interacting and note taking.

Paper and Pen or Laptop?

I use paper and pen to take notes whether or not I record. I write so sloppily at times, I have to type up my notes within two days while the material is fresh or my scribbles will become undecipherable. But I love holding pen to paper and letting my left hand go off on its own, capturing impressions, raising new questions, while I talk to my interviewee. I don't feel that with a laptop.

Here's what Sheryl says:

> No one can adequately write down an interview on pen and paper. This is super aged, and never was efficient. Either record it or use a laptop; we all type fast these days, so keeping up isn't an issue anymore — and if you miss something, you can ask your interviewee to please repeat. Also, if someone is talking real fast, you can politely ask them to slow down. This would apply whether you're trying to write it all down (again, that is so ancient) or you are recording.

Pick your preferred method. If you're not an expert typist you'll make lots of errors but it doesn't matter. The notes are for your viewing only and you'll clean up the portions that you use for your book.

Video Conferences

A fourth way to conduct interviews is by video conference over the Internet.

- Video conferences enable you to conduct interviews relatively inexpensively with people all over the world.
- Videos are more personal than phone or email because you can see who you're interviewing and what they're doing.
- You can record them — but ask for permission before you do.

You can set up your video conference using Skype, FaceTime, WhatsApp, Facebook Messenger, Zoom, BlueJeans, or any other software application that provides video calls for multiple users.

Follow Up

However you conduct your interview, as a courtesy, send your expert a brief email thank you note. Include the portion of your text with their answers and ask for an accuracy check.

It's always okay to revise an expert's quote to delete repetition, redundancy, and the "uh"s and "er"s that clutter our dialogue but are irritating in written form, as long as your final version is faithful to the original meaning. It is not okay to change the meaning.

In addition to gaining verification that your text is credible, you could gain a satisfied fan of your work who will give you a solid testimonial quote for your back cover — or a foreword.

Never be intimidated into changing your interpretation of information. But don't get caught having to defend a misquote.

When your book comes out, do send a complimentary copy with a signed note of thanks.

Ken Wachsberger

Organizing Your Interview Notes

You're going to interview a lot of experts for your book. You've got two ways to organize your notes and transcripts:

- Create one separate Word file for each interview and name them as I show you in "Name Your Files So You Can Find Them."

- Create one Word file for all your interviews and separate your notes and transcripts using page breaks, dates of entry, asterisks, or any other divider of your choice.

The first method is easier when you know whose interview you want to review. The second is easier when you know what was said but you aren' sure who said it, or you want to follow a path of interviews over a period of time.

Chapter 9

MOVING BEYOND MGS PARALYSIS

Are you a reluctant writer because you're no good at mechanics, grammar, and spelling (MGS)? Don't be.

John Steinbeck is my all-time favorite author. He could be serious and heavily political, as in *The Grapes of Wrath,* his classic story of migrant workers trying to find dignity and the American dream during the Depression era of the thirties. And he could be hilarious, as in *The Short Reign of Pippin IV,* his short satire on the French political system.

An Issue of Chicken and Egg

When I was writing my first novel, *Beercans on the Side of the Road: The Story of Henry the Hitchhiker,* whenever I got a mental block and didn't know where to go next, I could pick out any book from my vast Steinbeck collection, turn to any page, and start reading any paragraph. The way he could describe a man bending down on one knee, picking up a handful of sand from the beach, and watching it sift through the fingers of a softly folded fist was inspirational. I would read a page, maybe two, perhaps three if I was really stuck, and then cast it aside as my own ideas started to replace his in my consciousness.

And yet Steinbeck was a poor speller. Thank goodness for competent editors. (He wrote before the days of Spell-Check.) I bring up this Steinbeck anecdote to acknowledge a sad reality and make an important point:

- **The sad reality:** Although by the time students get to high school and college, they are assumed to be competent in mechanics, grammar, and spelling (MGS), in fact, many students, and adults, are not.

- **The important point:** Being deficient in MGS skills does not mean you can't be a writer, or aren't a writer already and don't realize it.

Don't ever think that because you stink at MGS you can't write. What comes first, the chicken or the egg? You can't correct your errors until you know what they are and you can't know what they are until you make them.

Excellent MGS skills are crucial to your making the desired impression on whoever reads your writing. But first write.

Then do the following and the skills will come:

- Ask your peers to pay special attention to those areas where you know you are weak (see "**Peer Reviewing with Honesty and a Base of Goodwill**"
- Get yourself a good grammar handbook and don't sell it when your book is finished.
- If you're affiliated with a school or university, drop in at its writing center and take advantage of its free tutoring services.
- Take a continuing education class.
- Hire an editor to review the final draft.

Common Errors

Here are the common errors I find in my students' and clients' papers. How many of them do you make?

- **Comma splices:** Separating two sentences with a comma instead of proper end punctuation: "It rained all day, I stayed inside." I never heard of them myself until I taught a course in basic writing to farm students at Michigan State University.

- **Run-on sentences:** The same as comma splices except that when the first sentence ends you go straight to the second with no end punctuation at all: "It rained all day I stayed inside." What is proper end punctuation: periods, exclamation points, and question marks.

- **Subject-predicate and antecedent-pronoun disagreement:** Historically a problem because of the English language's long tradition of having no recognized third-person singular neuter version of "they." But in recent years, the movement has been to accept "they" as both singular and plural. In March 2017, Associated Press editors announced that their stylebook would be "opening the door" to use of the singular "they" explaining that's how people speak anyway and there's no alternative. They provided the caveat that rewording is usually possible and always preferable. Sue Katz, author of *Lillian in Love,* celebrates its acceptance: "We feminist writers have been pushing for this for decades but it is now established use."

- **Passive voice:** Not necessarily an error, just weak writing. Example: "There were a lot of clouds in the sky" instead of "Clouds filled the sky." Avoid sentences beginning with any variation of "There is/are."

- **Spelling:** If you are unsure of your spelling, do a search on the way you think the word should be spelled and see how many times it comes up. If an alternate spelling has far more search results than your spelling, your spelling is probably wrong. Note also that the first entry on the first page is often a formal definition of the correctly spelled word. Finally, if you type a word and a squiggly line appears below it, check to see if you spelled it wrong. That method isn't airtight but it works often enough to keep an eye on. Here are some of the most common mistakes I find that Spell-Check won't catch:

  ◊   there/they're/their
  ◊   its/it's
  ◊   your/you're
  ◊   effect/affect
  ◊   then/than
  ◊   to/too/two
  ◊   a/an (it's "a honest" mistake)
  ◊   through/threw/thru
  ◊   foreword/forward (please, fellow authors, get this one right)

- **Alright**: All wrong

- **Etc.:** Used by academics when they can't think of anything else to say to make readers think they know so much more.

- **Pluralizing:** When did the plural of book become book's?

- **Clichés:** Avoid them like the plague.

- **Etc**.

Details, Details, Details

Remember, this is your book. You have the details in your head but your readers can only read what's on the pages. You're writing to communicate with them. You have to include enough specific details so they know what you're talking about:

Devon Hanover speaks positively about the methods of heart surgery you advocate in your workshop? Fine, but who is Devon Hanover? Oh, he's "director of cardiology at Sinai Hospital." That explanatory phrase answers a question you can anticipate your readers will have if you don't answer it in advance for them.

> **Hint #1**: Every time you introduce a new character, include a short phrase to introduce them:
>
> - Lou Winter, the president of the local teachers' union
> - Mary Katz, professor of business management
> - Here are some other ways to communicate with your audience: Be specific, not general; be concrete, not abstract.

For instance, you're telling a story about a surfer and it's 90 degrees out so you write, "It was a nice day." I picture zero degrees and white mountains because I'm a skier. You didn't communicate.

Hint #2: Avoid "nice."

Interpret this sentence: "The thing was uncomfortable wearing a thing around his thing." What I meant was: "The boy was uncomfortable wearing a tie around his neck." Is that what you guessed? If not, I didn't communicate.

Hint #3: Avoid "thing" (advanced writers also avoid "something," "nothing," "anything," and any other "thing" permutations).

Keep These Two Weapons in Your Arsenal

Finally, passion and facts alone won't win your written argument no matter how knowledgeable you are. You have to outmaneuver your opposition. Here are two weapons you can use in your writing, especially your essays, to make your arguments more convincing: anticipation/refutation and concession.

Weapon #1: Anticipation/Refutation

Imagine yourself the lawyer in a jury trial. You're presenting your closing arguments; then the other side will speak. Your opponent has been raising the same tired arguments for six months to support his case. You can poke holes in all of them. Yet, if you ignore them in your closing arguments and he presents them in his, you can't jump up at that time and say, "Yes, your honor, but…." You had your chance.

So, in your closing arguments, you anticipate that he will present his tired arguments and refute them: "When my opponent says this, remember that."

Or, think of writing an editorial for your local newspaper's Op-Ed page, the section on the editorial page where non-staffers get to express their opinions in essay form. As a non-staffer, you get one shot to present your arguments and then you have to allow other members of the community to respond. You won't get a second chance to present your case or rebut the other side. You have to do it right the first time.

Weapon #2: Concession

You believe passionately in your cause. But your opponent believes just as passionately in hers. The reason you have become so passionate is because you're faced with passionate opposition. On some level, whether you agree with her conclusions or not, there probably is some sound basis for her argument that you can concede is correct. It's not always easy. We want to stand firm against all opposition.

But remember the fable of the mighty oak tree and the small reed and recall that, while the oak stood firm against the wind until it was uprooted and destroyed, the reed swayed with the wind and stood upright again when it passed.

So, concede that your opponent has a point. Then render it ineffective: "She claims her data support the need to increase our defense budget, and she's correct. But her data were compiled by the arms manufacturer that financed her study."

In writing the traditional five-paragraph essay, the first paragraph, the introduction, states your thesis and the three main arguments supporting it. The next three paragraphs, the main body paragraphs, support the three main arguments in the order that they are presented in the introduction. Paragraph five, the conclusion, restates the thesis with a summary of the other three paragraphs, or repeats a key phrase from the introduction. When using anticipation/refutation and concession, give them paragraphs five and six and bump the conclusion back to paragraph seven.

Chapter 10

THE JOY OF DELETING, AND OTHER NEAT TIPS

Electronic technology has made revising text and correcting errors easier. If you don't understand the awesomeness of that statement, you didn't grow up before it was around.

Correcting Errors in the Typewriter Age

When I was in ninth-grade typing class, to calculate our typing speed, we would count how many words we typed on our portable Smith-Corona typewriters in five minutes, divide by five to figure out our words per minute, then subtract five words for every error, the premise being that it took you as much time to correct one error as it would have taken you to type five words. That formula was way generous. Our primary tool for correcting errors was the ink eraser, which looked like a pencil eraser but always ripped the paper by the time the erasure was complete.

Sometimes we were lucky to have in our possession a unique thin strip of correction paper with white powder on one side of it that you placed between any mistakenly typed letter on the paper and the ribbon, powder side facing the paper. Next, you would strike the corresponding key; the key would strike the strip; and powder would be released onto the paper, covering the incorrect letter and making it disappear. Then you would backspace one space and type the correct letter.

Voila! No error. For errors involving more than one letter, you would cover and delete every incorrect letter one at a time, then go back to the space where the first letter belonged and type the correct letters.

Ken Wachsberger

Improvements in Erasure Technology

But you paid a price. More powder was released than just enough to cover the error. Powder flaked freely. Every typist owned a brush and used it frequently to dust the keyboard so the powder wouldn't accumulate and cause the keys to stick.

That early correction paper was fine for correcting minor errors but what to do with a complete sentence? For that we used correction fluid, most often Liquid Paper, a white paint invented by the mother of the Monkees' Michael Nesmith that you brushed over the infected territory to make it disappear.

It was fast and easy but you had to wait until the liquid dried before you typed the correct word or else it would appear on the paper surrounded by an intrusive, slightly three-dimensional blob that rendered the letters blotched and unclear. Unfortunately, this was the only method for erasing long sentences or complete paragraphs. The trick was to use as thin a coat as possible, blow over the letters to speed-dry the process, and be patient.

And then came a miracle. It looked like the powdery correction paper but its surface appeared as a metallic film. When the key struck the back side, the front side released just enough of the film to cover the incorrect letter. No flaking occurred. It was considered a huge advance in the field of errors but still too time-consuming of a process for correcting longer passages.

The Revolutionary IBM Selectric

It was a special day when I moved beyond even that miracle and acquired my first IBM Selectric electric typewriter. The Selectric had two revolutionary features. First, in manual typewriters, the italics key didn't appear anywhere on the keyboard. To designate that text should be italicized, you underlined it; italics capability was a feature of typesetting equipment possessed only by the New York publishing houses.

The Selectric used metal balls, each with a different type style, or font, that you could attach to the computer by pressing and locking. You used some variation of the Courier font for most typing. Whenever a word had to be italicized, you would take off the Courier ball, put on the italics font, type the word, then switch balls. It was worlds ahead of the Smith-Corona.

The other feature was the internal correction paper capability that enabled you to backspace over the incorrect letter and type it with the feature engaged to delete it, then backspace again and type the correct letter. The complete process required four steps but only took a few seconds. Unless, of course, you were deleting a long word. Or a sentence. Or a paragraph. At some point, you had to use the white paint.

That's as good as it got in the typewriter age. Correcting errors always took effort and time. You let small errors slide and hoped the teacher or your editor didn't catch them. You didn't want to have to add a late-breaking paragraph on page 1 because when you typed that page over — from the beginning — the bottom paragraph would no longer fit. It would roll over, or reflow, to page 2, so you would have to type page 2 over. And what happened to the bottom paragraph on page 2?

Before making any major change, you would think, "Is this correction really worth it?" You submitted manuscripts that were "good enough" even when you knew they weren't.

Correcting Errors Today

Today, you have at least four ways to delete a word on your computer:

1. Place cursor after word you want to delete, hit Backspace to make it disappear, type correct word.
2. Place cursor before word you want to delete, hit Delete, type correct word.
3. Place cursor before word you want to delete, hit Insert, type correct word to cover word you want to delete.
4. Highlight word you want to delete with cursor, type correct word.

You can delete entire paragraphs by waving the cursor over the area you want to remove and hitting Delete.

No powder. No blobs. Almost no time.

Now when you insert a new paragraph on page 1, the bottom paragraph on the page automatically rolls over to the top of page 2, and the bottom paragraph on page 2 automatically rolls over to the top of page 3. It's seamless and paperless. You can edit and revise right up until deadline.

In fact, you don't even print out final pages. When you publish independently (aka self-publish), you send the electronic file as an attachment to your printer, along with the cover file, or upload the files for print on demand (POD) and ebooks. When you publish with another company, you submit the final manuscript as an email Word file attachment and they design the cover.

Other Essential Tricks That You Couldn't Do with the Typewriter

The Delete function is one of the inventions in the electronic era that have made life so much easier for writers. Another, Cut and Paste, I talk about in "Freewriting: Creating Order out of Chaos." Here are a few others that will make your writing and editing easier.

Track Changes

You can use Track Changes to edit faster and better. For instance, use it any time you're writing a new sentence to replace a current sentence that you think is weak but potentially salvageable. You don't want to lose the original in case it turns out to be better than the new. So, write your new text with Track Changes on and delete the current text. For comparison purposes, you'll still see it because Track Changes only strikes through the text and changes its color. If you decide you want to use the original text, just highlight the text and Reject Change.

As an editor, I edit clients' papers with Track Changes on so they can see every change I make. I send them two versions of every file, one with Track Changes on and one Clean, with all changes accepted. They read Clean for the flow. If they like what they read, they keep going. If they get to a passage that seems awkward or doesn't feel right, they refer to Track Changes. Any change that I make can be rejected to get back to the original version.

Find

When I finish my day's revising for any file, I write "[begin]" at the spot where I want to begin working the next day. The next day, I do a search for "[begin]" — my electronic bookmark — and I'm there. Sometimes you can just type "[b" and you'll get there.

When you're editing your final draft and you determine to replace all uses of "thing" that you wrote during freewriting with concrete nouns, searching "thing" will get you to every instance.

Find and Replace

When you discover that you've been alternately uppercasing and lowercasing a particular term and you want the manuscript to have consistency, spell the term with the case that you want it to have in both Find and Replace.

You can replace every use of the wrong case with the correct case instantly by hitting Replace All.

Or you can go one at a time, which is often necessary. For instance, most nouns are typed lowercase, but when they appear at the beginning of sentences they are uppercased. Replacing all uppercase spellings of the term with lowercase could create spelling errors that weren't already in the manuscript.

Are you still typing two spaces after the period? That custom was popular during the days when typewriters used monospaced fonts like Courier. With the rise in popularity of proportional fonts, like Times New Roman, the practice has become to type one space only. Typing two will only irritate your publisher.

You can instantly get rid of extra spaces between sentences by hitting the space bar twice at Replace > "Find what:" and hitting the space bar once at Replace > "Replace with:". Do the operation twice to your complete manuscript in case one instance had three spaces. It happens by accident and is easily corrected.

Make sure Track Changes is off during this operation.

Match case

If you want to search one case only, hit the "More > >" button on the Find and Replace screen and check the "Match case" box. When you're done, uncheck the box or the feature will remain.

PART 3: AS YOUR BOOK NEARS COMPLETION

Chapter 11

A FEW NOTES ON INDEXING

When you write a nonfiction book, the chances are good that you will include an index. If you publish through an established company, the chances are great that you will end up paying for someone to create it. Do you find the indexer yourself and pay upfront, or do you trust the publisher to be sensitive to costs that they're merely going to pass along to you anyway?

I prefer to handle the cost on my end because it gives me more control over the cost as well as the quality.

Roughly speaking, a trained indexer will charge $3 to $4 a page for general trade books and $4 to $5 a page for scholarly books; and complete a 200- to 300-page book in a week (if no overlapping projects are competing for time). Do the math: Your index will likely cost you between $600 (lowest rate, fewest pages) and $1,500 (highest rate, most pages) to complete.

If you want to do your own index, a regular license for the three main indexing software programs — Cindex, Macrex, and Sky Index — costs up to around $600, depending on what bells and whistles you're willing to purchase. Free trials are available for all of them; and Cindex has a student version for under $100.

A newcomer to the field, TExtract, comes in standard and professional versions for around $400 and $600 respectively. TExtract also offers single-publication author licenses for both versions.

If you're new to indexing you can count on needing two weeks to finish it.

If you cede that responsibility to the publisher but agree to eat the cost — which either will be paid up front by you or come out of your royalty, based on your negotiating skills with your publisher — insist on some version of the phrase "going rate." That phrase should find its way into any other clauses that obligate you to pay anything, such as to review proofs or format illustrations.

Do you live near a university that has a college of library and information science (formerly called library school)? If you do, ask the college dean if the faculty might include a professor who is passionate about your topic and would love the challenge of creating your index. Or ask for referrals to any Masters-level students whose livelihoods one day will include creating indexes for pay. They're looking for experience to build their portfolios. You can help one of them. It's a win-win.

Cost depends on your negotiating skills with your indexer and your indexer's love of your topic or need to build a portfolio. What service can you offer in exchange for your index?

In any case, I would feel confident in the ability of any professor or student whose name I obtained through a recommendation from the college dean.

For more on indexing software or finding a professional indexer, check out the website of American Society for Indexing (formerly American Society of Indexers) at www.asindexing.org.

Chapter 12

TRACKING DOWN EXPERTS FOR FOREWORDS AND
TESTIMONIAL QUOTES

As soon as you've got a working table of contents and a few polished chapters that represent your style and content, start thinking of experts whose kind words about your book will give it instant credibility and marketability.

Whose name or names would look good following the phrase "Foreword by" (please, not "Forward by")? Reach out to them. The tradition is to have one foreword per book but if you find two experts whose endorsements would each catapult your credibility to personal heights, go for them both. And get testimonial quotes from all the rest for the back cover and your book's website.

They're not that hard to find. No one is unreachable in today's connected world.

How It Used to Be

It didn't used to be this way. In 1992, I edited and published a 600+-page book that consisted of histories of individual underground newspapers from the Vietnam era of the sixties and seventies as written by key people on each of the papers. First, I had to find them so I could invite them to contribute their stories.

When I had begun work on the project four years before, I recalled my years as an editor and writer for *Joint Issue*, an underground newspaper from Lansing-East Lansing, Michigan during the early seventies. As a member of Underground Press Syndicate, we shared copies of every issue with the other members who shared theirs with us. *Joint Issue* received papers from all over the country. I read them all and was energized; it was from them that I selected the titles to include in my collection.

But I didn't know most of the writers and editors personally. Now I had to track them down to find one key person from each paper to write a history of that paper. Yes, it was common for academics to have campus emails. But many folks didn't yet have personal email, and social media didn't exist.

As good fortune would have it, I was now living in Ann Arbor, Michigan, seventy miles down the road from my Lansing-East Lansing home base of the seventies. In East Lansing, the Special Collections Library of my alma mater, Michigan State University, had a collection of underground papers from all over the country that was one of the best in the world. In addition, MSU Library had the distinction of owning the world's largest collection of phone books — remember them? Naturally they were located by the payphones.

So, I drove up there one day, found a place to park off campus so I wouldn't have to pay for parking, walked over to the library, and spent the first part of the day carefully perusing original copies of whatever papers from my list they had on the shelves. Dust floated off the pages of the papers as the librarian brought them to me. Carefully, so as to not rip the already-yellowing pages, I turned to the staff box of each paper and recorded in my notebook the names of every staffer who listed a first and last name. Then I went upstairs to research the phone books from the respective cities.

If I'm not mistaken, every phone book that I needed was in the collection. I looked up every name from my list to see if I could find anyone who wrote on any of the papers back when and was still around, and who had been insider enough to claim historian's rights or could connect me to someone who could,

When I found a match, I would call the related phone number and ask the person who picked up the phone, "Did you used to write for [title]?"

If the answer was yes, I introduced myself and asked, "Could you write an insider history of the paper or refer me to someone who could?"

You've Got the Time

Most often the person on the other end of the line was not the right person to write the history, but was able to connect me to someone who was, or someone who knew someone who was. I followed every trail, wrote down names of everyone I talked to, and took notes of conversations.

I had surprising success with this research method but it was a laborious, expensive process.

And Is It Easier Today?

Today, I could have located everyone I wanted to find, or someone who knew someone who knew someone who could connect me to them, on the Internet or through social media without leaving my home. So can you.

Internet

Good Internet research isn't always fast and easy. It takes patience and persistence. You experiment with keyword combinations while searching for other possible keywords.

Begin by just typing a name into whatever search engine you use. That doesn't always work — most likely a lot of others share the name of the expert you're trying to find. But sometimes that's all you need to do.

If it doesn't bring up the right person, or if it brings up so many links that references to your person are buried under irrelevant links, begin refining your search. Include the person's name in quotes followed by the institution where the person works, or the person's occupation, or an event that you associate with the person.

Sometimes you have to dig deep. I've found key information on pages ten and beyond of Google searches. Be sensitive to clues that will give you new search terms. Many have personal websites.

If you still can't find them, track down others who you know would know them: parents, children, friends, colleagues. Remember the six degrees of Kevin Bacon. Personally, I don't think it's more than five. What do you think?

Social Media

Or go straight to social media. I long ago lost track of how many experts I have found simply by searching on my favorite social media platforms, which have included Facebook, Twitter, and LinkedIn.

With Facebook and Twitter, you can send a brief private message of introduction. Offer to send much more detailed information in exchange for an email address. With LinkedIn, send a brief note requesting to connect so you can send more information. When you receive a connection, you also gain access to the email address.

Bottom Line

Everyone is accessible. Finding the phone number, email address, personal website, or social media account of the ideal person to write the foreword to your book or to give you a testimonial quote for the back cover is a reachable goal. Keep the vision and go for it.

Now What?

Once you've got the contact information, it's just a matter of introducing yourself and stating your request. If you have the email address, start there. Through email, you are creating documentation for your records, as well as templates to revise and reuse often. I prefer email first for all my communication.

If you don't have an email address but you have the phone number, call. Phone calling might seem like an intrusive way to make yourself known to a stranger so be extra polite and humble. Apologize freely. But don't expect an immediate yes without a manuscript review.

Assume instead serious interest. Request a current email address so that you can send a cover letter with more information and a few sample chapters. State your requested deadline. Make it as tight as necessary so that you can meet your self-imposed publishing deadline even if it arrives late. Your low-pressured approach will be appreciated.

You've Got the Time

Mailing your package through the postal service is my least-desired approach. It's expensive, it takes a long time, and, if they don't get back, you don't know if it got lost or ignored; in either case, your only recourse is to mail another package. Be sure to include a self-addressed, stamped envelope and keep researching for email and phone information.

Write respectfully to all your experts, as if they are real people, not gods and goddesses whose responses will make or break your career. Tell them who you are, what the book is about, why it is important to you, and why you would be deeply honored if they would write a foreword or give you a testimonial quote.

Speak from the heart. Don't ever offer up front to pay for the foreword. If someone asks for pay, decide how badly you want the endorsement and negotiate a deal.

But most foreword writers do not ask for pay or expect it, and testimonial quotes should not come with costs included. Attach — or enclose if you're sending through the mail — the table of contents, your author's introduction, and two or three chapters and tell them you would love to send the complete manuscript.

If You Don't Hear Back

With email, give two weeks for a response. If you don't hear back in that time, forward your original message along with the following new message:

Dear [Person Whose Quote I Want]:

Just a quick note to make sure you received the below message. I would be most grateful to hear from you.

Thanks in advance for your serious consideration.
Gratefully,

[Your Name]

The amount of time before you send your next reminder, if you still haven't heard back, has to be determined by your urgency to put your book to bed with that person's endorsement included. You don't want to be pushy but you don't want to give up. They have lives. Be patient. Begin the process as soon as you can, even before your manuscript is complete, so you don't have to be pushy.

But don't ever assume that because they don't get back to you they are rejecting your request. Write to them until you hear back. Assume your unanswered email requests merely got caught in the spam folder and try again. As much as your experts deserve patience, you deserve a response to a respectful request. You can handle rejection. You're a writer. But you need closure so you can plan your next step.

Whenever you decide to give them your next reminder, forward the same package that you sent two weeks before. Be sure to

- Delete the lines above "From:" in the message so it looks like a new message.
- Delete "FW:" on the Subject: line, for the same reason.

Or write a new letter and blame the spam folder for stealing your invitation.

Plan B

Meanwhile, be thinking of Plan B. Who is the expert you would next most like to write your foreword. Pull up your cover letter to Expert A (which you wisely saved in a logical folder on your personal drive and named so you could easily locate it; see "Name Your Files So You Can Find Them") and rename it to use it for Expert B.

But be sure to personalize it. The main body of your invitation will be similar from message to message and the table of contents that you attach will always be the same. But

- The reasons why you want each to be part of your book will differ, so you'll want to personalize the introduction to each letter.
- Various sections may have to be updated.
- Particular chapters in your book may appeal to one expert, other chapters to another expert. Send the chapters that will most appeal.

For instance, while I was recruiting testimonial quotes for my Voices from the Underground Series, Country Joe McDonald, leader of the legendary Country Joe and the Fish band from Woodstock fame, happened to visit the University of Michigan to perform. When I discovered he was coming to town, I pulled out my template testimonial-request letter and personalized a letter to him.

I knew Country Joe had served in the military in the sixties before becoming an antiwar leader and strong supporter of military veterans. So, I included, as one of my two chapters, the history of *Aboveground,* a military underground newspaper published by GIs out of Fort Collins, Colorado. An appendix to the story listed nearly 400 military underground newspapers from all branches of the military. At the time, that was the most exhaustive such list ever compiled.

After the concert, I introduced myself to Joe and gave him the package, which I asked him to read when he had the time. Joe wrote back I'm pretty sure within two weeks. In his response, he wrote:

> … an important project. That information needs to be available. I liked the list of GI newspapers and was not awarex there were so many.

Should You Write the Quote?

Some book coaches suggest you write the desired testimonial quote yourself, if that's what you're requesting, and ask the expert whose quote you want simply to agree to its authorship.

I disagree. It's easy, for sure. It enables the expert to give you a thumbs-up without much effort.

But you limit the potential awesomeness of the quote. I would never have had the nerve to write the rave reviews that many of my most admired testimonial givers gave me on their own and then asked them to approve it.

Shoot for the stars. You may not reach the stars but you'll reach far higher than if you shoot for the top of your roof and reach it.

If you've written a compelling cover letter, your table of contents is neat and well structured, your author's introduction is compelling, and your choice of chapters is wise, you will have given your expert enough to decide whether or not they will give you a quote. If you believe in your book and you think and act positively, it will likely come back better than you could make up.

By the Way

This chapter has been about how to find experts to write your foreword and testimonial quotes. Use it as well while you're doing research for your book. When you're looking for experts to bolster your arguments or fill in details of significant events, email interviews are easy, efficient, productive, and respectful of your experts' time limitations.

When they respond with brilliant answers to your compelling questions (which they will be because you read "Conducting Interviews"), you can use portions for authoritative quotes. If you have to modify a quote in any way from the original — usually to fit the flow of your text or to eliminate redundancy, never to change the intention of the author — run it by the expert for approval and clarification.

You establish credibility when you respect your experts. Later, if you want to ask them for testimonial quotes, you're already halfway there.

Chapter 13

THE BEST PROSE IS POETRY

I don't know how to compare the English language to other languages. I don't know which factors to compare or how they are judged. But when I'm writing a book I don't care. What I know is that English is a beautiful language and the best prose flows like poetry.

Does Your Prose Flow Like Poetry?

Does your prose flow like poetry?

We've already talked about how, while you're doing freewriting, you crank out every irrational fear of failure, every task to add to your to-do list, and every other thought that, if you don't write it down, will continue to fill space in your brain that your mind needs to cultivate fresh thoughts for your book.

By the time you finish your complete first draft, you will have long since gotten rid of them.

You've probably already answered those queries that you inserted in **[bold square brackets]**; or decided that you didn't need that material for your final draft and deleted the brackets unanswered.

But that weak writing — the "there is/are" sentences, repeated use of "thing," wordy sentences, and others — that entered your manuscript during the freewrite process are still there. Unless you've been paying attention to them.

Start paying attention to them early. Turning your prose into poetry isn't an onerous task that you complete at the last minute, like a college term paper.

Turning prose into poetry begins while you're reviewing your first freewrite. It's what you do in those five-minute bursts when you don't have time to develop a new thought; or at the end of a long day when you're too tired to write anything new but you can easily read and reread and re-reread what you wrote for the day.

That's when the artistry happens, when you have just enough time to combine two sentences to reduce choppiness and eliminate a few excess words; or just enough brain power left after a productive day to clarify a page of weak sentences so they make sense to someone other than you using as few words as possible.

Here is where your best artistic tendencies and anal-retentive compulsions flourish. "I'm on it," they say in unison.

Making Your Prose Flow Like Poetry

Here are twenty ways to make your prose flow like poetry, some of which I've already mentioned in different contexts, with explanations only if necessary or inspired:

1. Search for and replace every use of "thing" with a concrete noun. If a word means everything, can it mean anything?

2. Search for and replace variations of "There is" and "There are" with active verbs whenever possible (which is usually). For instance:

Instead of "There were a lot of protestors at the demonstration," how about "Protestors filled the streets and overflowed onto the sidewalks"?

The worst poetic sin of "There is/are" sentences isn't their occasional use but their recurring appearance, so often like a shotgun blast from a musket, back to back to back within the same paragraph.

3. Use Cut and Paste to move sentences until the order releases the flow of your idea.

4. Expand one-sentence paragraphs unless they are for emphasis or dialogue.

5. Vary your sentence structure to include a diverse sample of the three basic sentence styles:

- simple: subject noun and predicate verb
- complex: simple sentence and dependent clause, often separated by a comma
- compound: two simple sentences separated by a conjunction: "and," "but," "or," "nor," or "for," but not "however" or "though"

Combine short, choppy sentences to form smoothly flowing compound and complex sentences.

6. Eliminate redundancy: You repeated the same idea four times in the same paragraph because you were trying to figure out the best way to say it. Now get rid of the other three or combine elements of more than one, often by creating complex sentences.

7. Tighten up transitions between paragraphs, between sentences, and within sentences.

8. Check for consistency in verb tense and voice. If you're telling a story, you more often than not want to be in past tense.

9. Check for subject-predicate and antecedent-pronoun agreement: If you still believe that the English language doesn't have a third-person singular neuter pronoun to go with the plural "they," consider revising the sentence in plural:

"A student should do his/her/its homework" becomes "Students should do their homework."

Or try alternating masculine and feminine third person.

Ken Wachsberger

If you have joined the movement to declare "they" both singular and plural (see "Moving Beyond MGS Paralysis)" use "they." Whatever you do, be consistent.

10. Include plenty of colorful quotes to capture personalities, explain difficult concepts, and move the action. Don't just plop them onto the page. Use attribution: "she said"; "According to."

11. Spell your words correctly. Your book isn't social media. Readers will notice errors.

- If a word in your manuscript appears with a red squiggly line under it, you've probably spelled it wrong.
- Use Spell-Check. You might as well. It's on your computer. But don't settle for it. Spell-Check makes lots of mistakes, often because it doesn't understand your context.
- Make sure you're not mixing up the word you want with its homonym, another word spelled the same way but having a different meaning (see "Moving Beyond MGS Paralysis").
- And please don't pluralize a word by including an apostrophe before the "s": book > book's.

If you aren't sure how to spell a word, type the spelling you think into your Internet search bar and the correct spelling and dictionary definition will show up, often at the top of the first page, unless you're so far off you baffle Google, in which case keep guessing.

12. Do Search and Replace to turn two spaces between sentences into one. Run the operation twice in case you have three spaces between some sentences.

13. Sprinkle your text with figurative comparisons:

- Simile: Literary device that uses "like" or "as" to compare ideas or things that would not otherwise be considered comparable; in other words, "They're like apples and oranges."

110

- Metaphor: Considered stronger than simile because it gets right to the point by not using "like" or "as" — "They're apples and oranges."
- Analogy: Similar to metaphor and simile but requires explanation and usually leads to the conclusion that, if two ideas or things are similar in one way, they are similar in other ways as well. "Finding a good example of an analogy is a pain in the neck" is a good example of an analogy.
- Irony: A literary device that uses words with an apparent obvious meaning to mean the opposite, with "sarcasm" being irony with a bite. "Oh, yeah, that's a great example of irony!"

14. Avoid "nice": As meaningless to modify nouns as "thing" is to replace them. Use concrete, specific details to develop well-written sentences.

15. Replace weak verb following a string of adverbs with one strong verb.

16. Get rid of the qualifiers: very, somewhat, rather, quite a bit. What they scream is that you don't have confidence in the word that follows. Instead of "She was rather a bit lonely," what's wrong with "She was lonely"? Instead of "It's very cold," how about "It's freezing"?

17. Use the series of three: Wynken, Blynken, and Nod; Huey, Dewey, and Louie. Tom, Dick, and Harry. They flow. If you don't agree, you need to study your ABCD's.

18. "Alluring allocation of allegories" — I have no idea what that means but doesn't it flow nicely? It's called alliteration.

19. Raise the level of your vocabulary without sounding pretentious. Don't settle for the first word that comes to mind.

20. Use subheadings to break up the text and guide the flow of information.

In what other ways do you turn your prose into poetry?

Ken Wachsberger

Good Work

Don't submit your book for consideration or uploading until your prose flows like poetry. Revise and re-revise as many times as necessary until you can read it and exclaim, "This is amazing. I wish I had written it," and then realize you did write it. Congratulations. Your prose is poetry.

Chapter 14

PEER REVIEWING WITH HONESTY
AND A BASE OF GOODWILL

I was first drummer in my junior high school band. Always a highpoint of the school year was when we participated in competitions with other schools in the area. Impartial judges graded each band with some variation of "1" for the highest grade and "5" for the lowest. Most grades hovered in the 1-3 range. They were supplemented by individual comments from the judges.

Mr. Hollander Thinks He's Being Nice

On our bus ride home from one competition, our music teacher, Mr. Hollander, read aloud the judges' comments. All were surprisingly positive. But he didn't say anything about the drum section, which consisted that day of me.

"What did they say about the drums?" I asked. Mr. Hollander didn't respond. I asked again. He looked away as if he didn't hear me and began talking to another student.

I asked a third time. He finally answered. "The drummer needs to slow down and not get ahead of the other instruments," he read. Then he turned away.

What happened? What I believe is that he was trying to protect my feelings from being hurt by negative comments. Or maybe he was just ashamed because he had failed as a musician and a teacher.

What I know is that he deprived me of the opportunity to learn from my habit. How helpful might he have been if he had read their comments to me — privately, to avoid embarrassing me in front of the others, if that was his intention--and then worked with me in the following weeks to help me?

No Time to Be Nice

As a serious author with a completed manuscript, you want serious feedback as well. You've come this far. Now isn't the time to nickel-dime. A good editor is worth the investment.

But a good editor can be a costly addition to your budget. Editors generally charge by the hour or the word. You can keep billing hours to a minimum by giving your editor your cleanest possible manuscript.

So, once you've given it your best shot and before you submit it to your editor, share it with as many reviewers as you can. Invite peers, social media connections, clients, friends, relatives, and anyone else from your community to help you tear apart your book and put it back together.

Demand that they rebel against childhood. In those long-ago days, they, like you, probably learned, "If you can't say something nice, don't say anything at all?" Of course, they probably also learned, "Honesty is the best policy."

By the time you send them your manuscript, these two often-contradictory pearls of profundity have merged into "Honesty is the best policy unless you can't say something nice."

Here's the 1-2-3 of what nice looks like in the publishing world:

1. Your peer reviewers want to be nice and not hurt your feelings so they say they like your book even though major portions lack specifics and raise many questions that it doesn't answer.
2. You think, "Oh, they like it. It must be good," and send it to a publisher to consider for publication.
3. The publisher, who is paid to be honest, not nice, and who doesn't know you anyhow, says, "This stinks," and rejects it outright.

You've Got the Time

So how nice were your friends really being?

This is no time for them to be nice.

Sharing Your Manuscript

Send your manuscript as a Word file email attachment with Track Changes on so any revisions they make will be visible to you.

One reluctance others may have to accept your invitation is the fear that they don't know what to say. "I'm not a writer" is a common refrain.

So, help them out. Include a cover letter where you give them a bullet list of specific areas of concern. For example:

- How interesting was it?
- What questions did it raise but not answer?
- How convincing were the arguments I put forth?
- What passages were unclear or incomplete?
- How well did the sentences and paragraphs flow together?
- What grabbed you?
- What factual errors did you find?
- What grammatical errors did you find?
- Any other comments and suggestions?

Tell them to comment freely. Give them a deadline by which time you need to hear back from them.

Demand honesty with a base of goodwill and a commitment to find positive ways to critique, and they'll give it to you. "This stinks" is not acceptable. "I'm not clear what you mean by this" or "You said it was a nice day but I can't picture it; could you give me some specific details?" is.

Consider all comments — whether you implement them or not — with love, because some of them are going to hurt. But they will make your book better.

This book is a testament to that strategy, for which I thank Guy Kawasaki, whose book, *APE: How to Publish a Book,* introduced me to the idea.

Suggestion: Include reviewers in the acknowledgments section of your book.

PART 4: PUBLISHING YOUR BOOK

Chapter 15

CHOOSING YOUR ROUTE TO PUBLICATION

Now that your book is nearly finished, you need to be thinking more about publishing. Do you go the traditional route and give your book over to an established publisher? Or do you take advantage of current technology and publish it yourself? I've gone both routes. Each has pros and cons.

Becoming an Independent Publisher

In 1987, I went down to city hall in Ann Arbor, Michigan, paid $10, and became a Schedule C publishing company called Azenphony Press. Then I published my first book, *Beercans on the Side of the Road: The Story of Henry the Hitchhiker*. I typeset *Beercans* using WordPerfect 4.2. I was able to find a printer who agreed to charge me $1.33 per soft-cover book. However, I had to print 3,000 books.

Six years later, thanks to a cutting-edge technological process that enabled authors to print short runs of book titles at large-print-run unit prices, I published *Never Be Afraid: A Jew in the Maquis*, which I mentioned earlier. I typeset *Never Be Afraid* using WordPerfect 5.1, and printed a first run of 50 softcover books at $4 per book.

While the cost per book was more than it was for *Beercans*, I only had to lay out $200. As my friend Mel used to always say about the secret of success: "Cash flow." When I received an order for a book, I stuffed a copy from my basement or car inventory into a brown envelope, drove to the post office, and mailed it.

In 2015, I published the second edition of *Never Be Afraid*. Using current technology, I converted my WP 5.1 manuscript file to Microsoft Word and updated the manuscript. Then I published it through Azenphony Press as both an ebook on Smashwords and Amazon and a softcover print on demand (POD) on Amazon.

Both services, Smashwords and Amazon, were free. To get to Amazon, the PODs were printed at CreateSpace and sold on Kindle, both of which were owned by Amazon. When orders came in, Smashwords and Amazon handled all fulfillment and shipping.

CreateSpace Absorbed by Kindle

Or at least that's how it was until August 2018 when a joint press release from the two Amazon subsidiaries announced that CreateSpace was being absorbed by Kindle and they were now, in effect, "a single entity." Files that authors once uploaded onto CreateSpace to get their books sold on Amazon they would now upload directly onto Kindle.

As one CreateSpace representative explained to me, Kindle Direct Publishing (KDP) was now "the single place to publish and manage your paperback and digital books. On KDP, your paperbacks will still be printed in the same facilities, on the same printers, and by the same people as they were on CreateSpace."

Books and author information were transferred automatically and, she promised, any sales during that time would be seamless and uninterrupted. No royalty payments would be missed. However, they would now be sent every sixty days instead of every thirty days.

The first edition of *You've Got the Time* was my first POD uploaded directly to KDP. Amazon handled fulfillment and shipping. Smashwords and Amazon competed for ebook sales.

D2D-Smashwords Merger

Then, on March 1, 2022, Draft2Digital merged with Smashwords. The new company was named Draft2Digital. I embraced the potential and am learning how to take advantage of it.

You've Got the Time

I'll be distributing my ebooks and PODs with the new Draft2Digital. Their vast network will send my book onto every network I want it to go and more, including Amazon, Barnes & Noble, and every network where IngramSpark distributes.

Amazon still also distributes my ebooks.

Ebooks and PODs are available for purchase everywhere in the world every day of the year, 24 hours a day, using any search device. The success or failure of my books and how I get to use them is totally up to me. I pay all expenses but I reap any rewards and I have no limitations on how I may use my intellectual property.

The Traditional Alternative

Are traditional publishers obsolete?

Of course not. Publishing with them still has advantages:

- They pick up most of the costs for editing, design, typesetting, printing, fulfillment, and distribution.
- They can attract big-name endorsements for their books (but so can you if you read "Tracking Down Experts for Forewords and Testimonial Quotes").
- They are more likely to get their books translated into different languages or turned into movies.
- They provide better distribution through print bookstores.
- You have a better chance of getting an advance — which in the academic market is often more than all the royalties you'll ever receive.
- You can derive a certain status from having the imprint of an established publisher on your book.
- If you are an academic on the publish-or-perish treadmill, your tenure committee may not count your independently published book.

But you pay a price. I won't go into detail about the traditional author boilerplate contract here. I've saved that for Part 6, which is all about author contracts, including how to negotiate a better one. Suffice it to say here that the traditional boilerplate contract is written by the publisher's lawyer for the sole benefit of the publisher. It treats the author as a competitor rather than a partner and is designed (whether intended or not) to crush the spirit of the author and remove them from the marketing and sales process, a foolish strategy given that the author has the most energy invested in the book and has the most long-term interest in its success.

Many boilerplate contracts, especially in academia, steal the author's copyright in exchange for a tiny royalty and then require the author to pay so many costs that the author's best outcome is to lose money in exchange for a byline. They don't allow authors to resell their own books and they never technically go out of print so authors can never regain their rights.

Finding a Publisher

There's more. But don't get me started here. Check out Part 6 and know that, if you are able to negotiate a decent contract, you can do well with an established publisher, especially if you develop a relationship with the in-house editor, who often is an author like you. To find a publisher:

- Get familiar with *Writer's Market* and *Literary Marketplace,* the two major sources for listing publishers, their contact information, what they are looking for in books and clients, and how to approach them.
- Study publisher lists that you discover through Internet searches.
- Browse the aisles of bookstores to see what other books are on the same shelf where your book would go and see who published them.
- Do an Internet keyword search and see what books come up and who published them.
- Attend writers' conferences and visit publisher exhibit tables or sit in on sessions where publishers speak.
- Read publishers' websites, see what genres they publish, and send them what they want. Most often you'll send it all electronically. If you send it via postal mail, include a self-addressed, stamped envelope.

You've Got the Time

Approaching a Publisher

Every publisher has unique instructions as far as what variations and component parts of your complete manuscript they want to see and in what format before they will consider you.

But every book package will include a cover letter in which you

- Provide an overview of the book
- Introduce yourself and your qualifications to write the book
- Explain its concept and purpose
- Identify your competition
- Describe your marketing plan
- Share any testimonials you have already received

Attachments to the cover letter may include

- Table of contents
- Chapter summaries
- Sample chapters

Check their website and read their instructions to learn what information they need from you and what items they want you to send. If you have any questions, call them and talk to a real person.

Finding an Agent

A good literary agent can help you connect with publishers who would otherwise be unapproachable. In fact, many, but not all, publishers only take submissions from agents. An agent can help you to negotiate bigger advances, higher royalties, and wider distribution through multiple channels. Unfortunately, some agents only accept manuscripts from authors who have already been published by major houses.

To find an agent:

- Get familiar with *Writer's Market* and *Literary Marketplace*, which also have information about agents including which ones will work with new writers, what genres they handle, and what to send them in your introductory package.
- Read author introductions and acknowledgments of similar books to learn names of their agents, who may want to represent your book as well.
- Attend writers' conferences and visit their tables or sit in on their sessions.
- Read agents' websites and send them what they want. As with publishers, most often you'll send it all electronically. If you send it via postal mail, include a self-addressed, stamped envelope.
- Seek personal introductions from author friends who have agents whose interests appear compatible with your book.

If an agent asks for an upfront reading fee, run in the other direction. Likewise don't let them even suggest placing you with a subsidy, or vanity, press.

For more information on agents, check out Richard Curtis' *How to Be Your Own Literary Agent: An Insider's Guide to Getting Your Book Published*, now in its revised fourth edition (see "**Further Resources**").

A Viable Option and a Bonus Tip

Today, negative connotations of self-publishing have been vanquished as more and more authors are setting themselves up as licensed independent publishing companies at their local city halls and publishing high-quality, well-designed, carefully edited books themselves.

You can do that, too. It's a viable, respectable option, as long as your book is well edited and carefully crafted. Understand also that the commercial and critical success or failure of your book is totally up to you.

But if you go the traditional route and you are fortunate enough to find yourself looking at a contract, join the National Writers Union immediately before you sign it. Then ask to talk to a book contract adviser (see "Negotiating Your Book Contract").

While you're at it, ask about NWU's National Writers United Service Organization (NWUSO), another way you can solicit tax-deductible donations to support your book.

Chapter 16

ORDERING THE FRONT MATTER AND BACK MATTER

When you publish through another company you don't give much thought to designing the copyright page or assigning an ISBN. Those tasks fall to the publisher, who also arranges for the book to be copyrighted, whether in the publisher's name or yours — depending on how savvy you were in your negotiations.

Publishing with Another Company

You'll write your own author's introduction (also called preface); the dedication, to whomever or whatever inspired you during the writing of your book; and the acknowledgments page, where you thank everybody who gave you support and encouragement along the way. You'll format the table of contents. And you'll track down and invite someone with credibility in your field to write the foreword (see "Tracking Down Experts for Forewords and Testimonial Quotes").

They go in the following order:

- Dedication
- Table of Contents
- Foreword
- Author's Introduction
- Acknowledgments

If you want to begin the book with a quote that captures the essence of your entire book, it goes between the dedication and the table of contents and is called the epigraph.

These items are all elements of the front matter, the pages that precede page 1 of your manuscript. There are other elements but, because you found another publisher, you don't have to worry about them.

Back matter includes any appendices and lists of additional sources that you created or compiled to add value beyond your main text; and an index, whose costs you will foot unless you can negotiate for the publisher to cover them (see "A Few Notes on Indexing").

Publishing Independently

When you publish independently as a POD, you have to add those front matter elements that we ignored above:

- Book half title
- Series title, frontispiece, or blank
- Title page
- Copyright page

For ebooks, independent publishing guru Guy Kawasaki suggests the following abbreviated elements to follow the cover:

- Blurbs
- Table of contents
- Foreword or preface (but not both, nonfiction only)

That's it. And then go right into chapter 1.

Working with Sampling

Those other traditional elements of the front matter, Guy suggests, you can put in the back so that potential readers who want to sample your book can get to the main text sooner and see more of it than of the front matter.

Sampling is a voluntary percentage of the book that you will allow the platforms that sell your book to make freely available to viewers. It is a concept in the electronic world comparable to browsing in the print world, except that in the electronic world, you can limit the number of pages viewers may browse.

Whatever percentage you choose, you want as many of those pages as possible to be main text, not front matter. No one ever bought a book because of an alluring copyright page.

One feature of your POD's back cover is testimonial quotes, or blurbs. Ebooks don't have back covers so, suggests Mark Coker, creator of Smashwords, put them all the way in front and title the page "What Others Are Saying about [Your Title]." Keep them short and do not use too many, again, so samplers can get to the main text more quickly and see more of it.

Upgrade Your Back Matter

Coker suggests sprucing up the back matter by adding some promotional elements:

- Final Word to Readers: Thank your readers for reading your book; encourage them to write an honest online review.
- Call to action: Next steps after finishing your book, like checking out your website or signing up for your newsletter.
- About the Author: Introduce yourself to your readers.
- Other Books By: Include URLs (POD) or live links (ebook) to your website or your other books.
- Connect with Me Online: Links to your social media sites and Smashwords/Draft2Digital author page. (You'll want to change that to your Amazon author page and change the file name before uploading to Amazon.)
- Instructions on how to purchase in bulk at discount off cover price.
- Samples of another book: For you fiction writers whose novels fall within the same genre, this is a great way to plug your upcoming book.

Check Mark Coker's *The Smashwords Style Guide* and Guy Kawasaki's *APE: How to Publish a Book* in "Further Resources" for specific formatting and uploading instructions that are beyond the scope of this book.

Chapter 17

DESIGNING THE COVER

I showed you earlier (see "Ordering the Front Matter and Back Matter") that you can't use the same inside text files for both PODs and ebooks because of variations in the order of items in the front matter and back matter.

You'll need two cover files also, but for a different reason: While the two front covers are the same, ebooks don't have back covers. That's why the blurbs that appear on the back cover of your POD appear in the front matter in your manuscript.

Also, like butterflies, they don't have a spine.

Do It Yourself or Farm It Out

If you have artistic skills or desire, you can design your own cover by uploading photos and images from your personal collection or that you purchased at online services like canva.com.

But beware the simplicity of the process and don't do it yourself to save a buck. As Mark Coker, founder of Smashwords, now chief strategy officer at Draft2Digital, warns:

> Readers judge books by their cover. If your cover doesn't grab the attention of the right target reader, your book will sell poorly. If it grabs the attention of the wrong reader, what sales you earn will lead to poor reviews. A good cover, through its imagery alone, makes an aspirational promise to the book's target reader. Although most authors will tell you they understand the importance of a great cover, I'm constantly surprised by the large number of self-

published authors who publish books with homemade covers that look homemade.

He encourages you to let a professional cover designer handle the task if you aren't one yourself:

Readers expect your cover to look as good as or better than what the large, traditional publishers are putting out. Traditional publishers create fantastic covers because they use professional cover designers. Professional cover design need not be expensive. You can find great ebook cover designers for under $300.

Dave Bass uses Adobe Photoshop or Indesign to build his covers because they enable him to use image-building "layers." Dave is a self-labeled street mechanic who taught himself design and formatting while working as a shop steward and community organizer.

For KDP we get a template from the KDP Cover template generator. To minimize issues, whether with KDP or IS, respect the POD template! For custom book cover sizes not covered by the KDP cover template generator we've used Bookow.

Images he uses are 300 dpi and are submitted in the CMYK color space. "KDP will accept images in the RGB color space, but I don't think IngramSpark does. Also, I feel CMYK may give a more accurate idea of the physical result as that's the color space used by printers."

PDFs for interior files and cover files should comply with the standard PDF/ X-1a:2001.

An alternative to doing it yourself or hiring a professional graphic designer is to try Draft2Digital's wraparound process to create your own. As Coker notes, "The same general principles apply. D2D starts with the author-provided ebook cover (front cover only, as is the case with ebooks) and then their technology can extrapolate it into a spine image and back cover image." I introduce it to you in "Uploading Your POD to Draft2Digital" so I won't go into detail here beyond saying it is a worthy and interesting alternative.

You've Got the Time

Write Your Own Text

If you choose to farm out the cover design to a professional designer, be as clear as possible about what kind of image you want to convey through photos, pictures, typeface, and color.

And definitely write the text, or at least have a strong hand in it.

I introduced you earlier to two of my marketing gurus, Mark Coker and Guy Kawasaki. Another is Dan Poynter, one of the first generation of independent book publishing gurus, who we lost in 2015.

In designing your front cover, Guy says, make sure that

- the title uses typeface large enough that when your book appears online as an icon, the title is still readable; and
- the cover makes Internet browsers take a second look instead of flipping through to the next page.

Dan divided the back cover into three parts, from top down:

- a paragraph or series of bullet points that market your book through a brief but compelling description under an equally compelling title
- three or four testimonial quotes that give your book credibility and marketability
- a brief author bio with optional photo on the bottom left; your ISBN barcode on the bottom right (see "Get Your Own ISBN and Barcode")

For more specific information on designing book covers, I refer you to Dan's *Dan Poynter's Self-Publishing Manual* and Guy's *APE: How to Publish a Book*, both of which will take you far beyond the limits of where I can take you. Complete citations are in "Further Resources."

Chapter 18

GET YOUR OWN ISBN AND BARCODE

The ISBN, or International Standard Book Number, is the number that identifies your book or audiobook from among all the others. Libraries order books by ISBN. So do grocery stores and bookstores, which get discounts so they can resell them and make a profit for their service.

Some platforms — CreateSpace did; Kindle Direct Publishing and Draft2Digital do now — offer free ISBNs as a convenience. Remember that not all conveniences are free. ISBNs are assigned by publisher. When you allow your platform to assign their own ISBN, you are in effect allowing your book to appear in Books in Print as if they are the publisher.

Kindle Direct Publishing now offers a slight nuance. As their customer service representative told me, "We will register your book's imprint name as 'Independently published' with Bowker (the US ISBN agency), and this information will also be displayed on your Amazon detail page."

However, "Free KDP Print ISBNs can only be used for books published on KDP Print."

You can do better. Get your own ISBN.

Ordering Your ISBN

Here's what you do.

Contact R.R. Bowker, the keeper of the ISBNs in the United States, at http://www.bowker.com and go to their Publishers page.

It's been over thirty-five years since I founded Azenphony Press and obtained one hundred ISBNs. I don't remember there being any cost at all. If there was, it could not have been much because I couldn't have afforded that many at today's prices.

You can order ISBNs in quantities of 1 ($125), 10 ($295), 100 ($575), and 1,000 ($1,000). Purchase according to your publishing vision but remember that for every book you publish you need an ISBN for every format in which the book appears. Yes, hardcover and softcover versions require separate ISBNs. Your ebook and audiobook require two more.

The only exception: A book format that you plan to upload onto different platforms can use the same ISBN.

In the first edition of *You've Got the Time*, I noted that a second edition traditionally warrants a new ISBN. However, I warned, in the e-world, whatever online reviews you attract for your first edition will be wiped out if you create a new ISBN for the second edition. So, keep the same ISBN for subsequent e-editions.

I no longer believe this to be true. As I show in "Preserving Reviews in Subsequent Editions on Amazon," you can preserve your reviews when your book moves into a new edition with a new ISBN.

If you are planning to publish one book as a POD and an ebook, you need two immediately. Purchasing two individually comes to $250, which is $45 less than the cost if you buy ten at a time. If you go audio, you'll need a third so you're already over the cost to buy ten at once.

How many additional books do you see yourself publishing? Purchase ISBNs for them now to take advantage of quantity discounts. If you plan to publish other authors besides yourself, you'll surpass ten ISBNs quickly. For less than double the cost of the first ten, you get another ninety.

Don't be afraid to stretch yourself. You never thought you'd write one book and now you're preparing the final draft for publication. Who says you can't write another?

The ISBN Barcode

Once you've got the ISBN, converting it to a barcode is essential — for your POD only — and with good reason: Resellers of your book are going to want to record the sale by scanning the back cover at the cash register.

Scanning the barcode eliminates the need for the cashier to write or type your ISBN. It's faster. It's more accurate. It makes taking inventory far simpler and reduces employee training time.

The good news is, conversion is simple thanks to the availability of free conversion tools on the Internet. Just do a Google search for "barcode generator" and use the first link that's free and works.

Or, if you leave white space on the bottom right-hand corner of the back cover of your POD where the barcode goes and upload the cover to Kindle Direct Publishing or Draft2Digital, it will come back to you with the barcode filling the white space, at no cost to you.

Chapter 19

MANUSCRIPT SUBMISSION AND CODING YOUR FILES

When you first approach a traditional publisher, it won't be with a complete manuscript. Every publisher will have its own submission criteria, which you can read off their website. Most will involve some variation of

- a table of contents,
- an overview of the complete book, and
- two or three sample chapters, all sent as Microsoft Word doc file attachments to
- a cover letter of one or two pages that explains what the book is about, why you are qualified to write it, and how you plan to help promote and sell it.

You don't have much negotiating power at this time. If instructions require you to send hard copy, you send hard copy. No coding for uploading is involved.

Manuscript Submission in the Traditional Publishing World

But if you sell them on your book proposal and you are fortunate enough to receive a boilerplate contract, see if under "Manuscript Submission" there is a clause that says some variation of "Author will submit two manuscript hardcopies and one electronic version." If it does, cross out "two manuscript hardcopies and" and initial the change. Remember, you're still in the negotiation stage here. You can refuse that ridiculous request.

And your editor probably won't even care. No reputable editor edits off hard copy anymore. Good chance it's a phrase left in the boilerplate from the pre-digital era and the lawyer just never revised the contract for the times. For you, it's a waste of paper, packaging, postage, and precious time. Ecologically it leaves a huge footprint.

That's manuscript submission in the traditional publishing world.

Manuscript Submission in the Independent Publishing World

If you are planning to publish independently, you need to select your platforms to produce and distribute your book. To begin, do you turn your book into an ebook or a print on demand (POD)?

The answer to that question is simple: Do both (and consider an audiobook also; we'll discuss audiobooks later). You've got readers in both venues. Why limit yourself? This isn't about which methods you prefer; it's about which methods your readers prefer.

Every platform has its own unique author contract. I won't try to cover each one here. What I will do instead is give you some general words of wisdom that you can apply to every contract:

- Make sure the agreement is not exclusive. In other words, if you realize later that you can get a better deal somewhere else, or another platform will enable you to reach a whole new audience, you aren't limited to the lesser deal.
- Don't let it take away your copyright.
- Make sure your POD contract gives you the right to buy books for inventory at a low enough price that your selling price can cover expenses and leave you with money for promotion.
- It should have an escape clause so you can get out of it whenever you want.
- It should not charge you to use it.

And always remember that your POD or ebook platform is not your publisher. They are a printer for your POD and a distributor for your POD and ebook.

You are your own publisher:

- If one claims otherwise, run from it.
- Reject any offers to accept "free" ISBNs and instead spring for your own (see "Get Your Own ISBN and Barcode").

How I Did It

This section begins my personal journey to independent publishing. I share what was in order to show how comparatively simple it has become since the merger of Draft2Digital and Smashwords. If you want to skip it and go straight to how simple it is now, you can begin at "How I Do It Now."

I Started with Smashwords

Before the merger, I sold my ebooks primarily through Smashwords and Amazon.

I liked Smashwords immediately because founder Mark Coker is a writer who created a writer-friendly platform to distribute ebooks (see "Selling Ebooks: An Interview with Smashwords Founder Mark Coker"). He regularly posts blogs and offers website promotions to help Smashwords authors sell more ebooks. Earlier I mentioned *The Smashwords Book Marketing Guide,* his free ebook of so many suggested ways to promote books, I still haven't absorbed them all.

I also liked that he paid royalties monthly even if the amount owed the author was as low as a penny (see "You're Screwed No Matter What You Do – but You Can Make It Better"). To put that into perspective, traditional publishers not uncommonly will withhold royalties until the cumulative amount due has exceeded an arbitrarily high bar, often more than $50.

Enter the Behemoth

And Amazon is the behemoth that you can't ignore.

- Books uploaded to Smashwords automatically were distributed through Apple iBooks, Barnes & Noble, Kobo, and Scribd, as well as a growing list of other retailers and public libraries.
- Books from Kindle Direct Publishing, which is owned by Amazon, are distributed directly to consumers through the complete Amazon network including Amazon.com and Amazon Europe.

For softcover PODs:

- Kindle Direct Publishing again but not Smashwords, which printed only ebooks.

Amazon offers a resellers discount to bookstores that want to purchase your book to resell. However, bookstores hate working with, or through, Amazon, whose middleman status cuts into their profits.

The Behemoth Alternative

They prefer actual book wholesalers, especially Ingram, the largest, which gets books into 39,000 online and brick-and-mortar retail stores and libraries. For libraries, you want Baker & Taylor also for your print books.

- IngramSpark, which is owned by Ingram, has been the go-to distributor for getting your PODs and ebooks into both distribution networks as well as Amazon.

So, it was important for me to get my books onto IngramSpark to attract bookstore and library sales.

POD covers for IngramSpark may be hard or soft, flexibility that Amazon did not have when the first edition of this book appeared but does now.

IngramSpark charges $25 for ebook title setup and $49 for combined ebook and print setup but offers occasional no-fee opportunities and refunds the setup fee if you purchase fifty copies in the first sixty days after publication. While Amazon does not distribute outside the Amazon network, IngramSpark is able to get books onto the Amazon network.

Coding and Uploading Your Files

To get onto Smashwords with your ebook, all you needed to do was code your Word files to fit the formula that Coker created.

- For the techno-savvy among us who are comfortable coding files themselves, he provided complete instructions in his free ebook, *The Smashwords Style Guide.* More power to you.
- For the rest of us, he created "Mark's List," a free list of graphic artists, authors, and techno-geeks who have successfully coded books onto Smashwords and are now offering their services to others at incredibly reasonable rates.

I found my current typesetter, Cal Sharp from Caligraphics, on "Mark's List." Cal has designed and coded main text and cover files for me ever since; and he has tweaked cover files and turned them into business cards, postcards, and bookmarks.

The Word file that Cal created for my Smashwords ebook main text was so similar to the Amazon file that he included them both in the same package. The big difference between the two: the Smashwords edition made reference to itself potentially up to four times as being the "Smashwords edition":

- On the inside cover page below the title, where you write "Smashwords Edition";
- At the top of the copyright page, where you write "Published on Smashwords by" and then your company name;
- At the bottom of the copyright page, where you include the "Smashwords Edition License Notes" (see *The Smashwords Style Guide)*; and
- In the suggested back matter section, "Connect with Me Online," where you include links to your social media sites and Smashwords author page.

Cal deleted the first three of those references and replaced the Smashwords author page with my Amazon author page for the fourth, renamed the file, and I was just about ready to upload onto Amazon.

According to Cal: "One more thing to be aware of: If you format your paragraphs flush left, with no first line indent, Kindle will sometimes indent the first line anyway. The workaround is to set the first line indent to 0.01" in the paragraph style, which Kindle will do, and it'll look flush to the reader."

I followed the simple instructions on the respective websites to upload my files.

Uploading to IngramSpark

I uploaded my files to Smashwords and CreateSpace [now Kindle] myself. I balked at using IngramSpark because I didn't like that they charged. But I believe booksellers don't want to work with Amazon and I support independent booksellers. So, when IngramSpark offered a coupon for free setup, I made sure I got in under the deadline.

But I delegated the task of uploading files to my friend, Dave Bass, who warned me that the covers might require tweaking:

> IS uses a cover template that is slightly different from KDP, so I'll obtain the IS cover template. Then, in Photoshop, I place the cover over the IS template layer by layer, adjusting elements like images or text (title, author name, etc.) as needed.

I knew Dave, who I introduced you to earlier, could do it faster and better than I could and would get it done before the coupon's expiration date and at a reasonable rate.

I sent Dave the following electronic files:

- Ebook: the ebook front-only cover file, which I also used for Amazon and Smashwords; and the Amazon inside text, which didn't make references to itself the way the Smashwords file did.
- Soft cover: the two CreateSpace/Kindle files for inside text and front-and-back cover.

You've Got the Time

What we both thought would be an easy process became complicated when IngramSpark charged that my ISBNs were already in use on other books. Of course, they were, we said: the same books that sold on Smashwords and Kindle.

But, we learned, I had placed my books in KDP's "Expanded Distribution," where books swim in the same distribution waters as do IngramSpark books. Before I could go live with my PODs on IngramSpark, I had to take my books out of Expanded Distribution and submit a title transfer form for each book.

It was a frustrating process that should not have been so complicated but we got everything completed before the coupon expired. They even tweaked my cover files to fit their template.

I was able to use the same interior files for both versions.

But what about my ebooks, which the coupon from IngramSpark didn't mention? Here's Dave's analysis:

> To get ebooks onto IngramSpark you would have to either upload an ebook in epub format (NOT the formats used by Amazon Kindle) or have IngramSpark convert your print pdfs at 60 cents a page.... I think IS also charges a $25.00 setup fee for each ebook.... If you have ebooks on Amazon Kindle, I'm not sure it's worth doing ebooks through Ingram. The last statistic I saw indicated that Amazon Kindle had 83% of the US ebook market.

So, I kept my ebook files off IngramSpark and uploaded them only to Kindle and Smashwords. My POD went onto Kindle and IngramSpark.

How I Do It Now

Then Smashwords merged with Draft2Digital. I was relieved and pleased to learn that D2D would be preserving Smashwords' policy of paying penny royalties.

Suddenly, Smashwords users inherited the ability to create softcovers through D2D, where softcovers were in beta testing. It got even better on March 14, 2023, when D2D announced that "D2D Print just opened up for every author, everywhere." In other words, they passed the beta test.

Through the merger, Smashwords became part of D2D's distribution network, which includes Amazon, Barnes & Noble, Kobo, Scribd, Apple, Tolino, Overdrive, Bibliotheca, 24Symbols, Baker & Taylor, Hoopla, Vivlio, and Palace Marketplace.

The Policy with Softcovers

Because the network includes Amazon, I no longer need to upload my files to Kindle to sell my books on Amazon. (For an exception, see "Preserving Reviews in Subsequent Editions on Amazon.")

D2D gets books into the same stores as IngramSpark, so I no longer need to upload to IngramSpark.

Added bonus: D2D promises to tweak the cover files to satisfy every platform's idiosyncrasies!

The Policy with Ebooks

The policy with ebooks is confusing and unclear. The D2D-Ingram contract does not apply to ebooks so, I thought, I should have been able to upload my ebooks to D2D and Kindle both.

In fact, I was told by D2D IT, "For ebooks, Amazon doesn't use an ISBN, they assign their own ASIN, so the same ISBN can be used for ebooks across all vendors. Not so for print books."

I agreed.

But when I tried to opt in to Amazon distribution, I was warned, "Don't select Amazon distribution if your book is already available in digital form at Amazon."

You've Got the Time

When I uploaded previous ebooks on Smashwords and Kindle, and when I uploaded previous softcovers on Kindle and IngramSpark, I never had this problem. Why now and since when?

In the end, I opted out of Amazon for my ebook on D2D and got there through Kindle in order to preserve my reviews from the previous edition; I opted in everywhere else, as I was commanded, but I don't understand why this is necessary.

* * *

Those are the platforms that I use. Newer ones may be better. Find the ones that work for you.

As they say in the banking industry: Diversify. That's why you don't sign exclusive book author contracts and you keep your copyright.

Chapter 20

UPLOADING YOUR POD TO KINDLE

A benefit of using Draft2Digital is you can submit one set of metadata and upload one set of files and they will get your book onto every major platform they serve. You can bypass Kindle altogether and still get your books on Amazon through D2D.

However, if your book is a revised edition of a book you previously uploaded to Amazon and you want to get onto Amazon this time through D2D, Kindle can't link the book pages from the two editions and you will lose the reviews you attracted from the earlier edition.

To preserve your reviews on Amazon, you will have to upload your ebook files twice, once to Kindle for Amazon distribution and once to D2D for distribution everywhere else.

In "Preserving Reviews in Subsequent Editions on Amazon," I show you how to link editions on Amazon so you don't lose your reviews.

In this chapter and the next, I show you how to upload your files onto Kindle and Draft2Digital, the two platforms I use because they distribute my book on every major electronic network and are so easy to maintain.

Getting Started with Kindle

Registering and uploading your book on Kindle is a simple process that takes only a few minutes.

Here's what you do:

1. Set up your KDP account and sign in. You will be taken to your bookshelf.

2. Click +Create and be taken to a page that asks you what you would like to create. Your options are ebook, POD, hardcover (which is still in beta format as of this writing), a series page, and Kindle's new Vella version. You can only do one at a time.

   I chose to start with paperback for *Never Be Afraid*. The instructions are the same for the others so I won't spell them out here.

   Series and Vella options are for a later date, maybe but not now. The Vella option, which is new to Kindle, is for those of you who want to publish serialized stories one episode at a time.

Paperback Details

On the next page, your "Paperback Details" page, I noted my book's title and that it was in English. I added that I co-authored it with Bernard Mednicki, the hero of the story; and that this was the book's third edition.

I pulled the description from the book page of the second edition and edited it down.

> "Never Be Afraid: A Belgian Jew in the French Resistance" is the powerful, poignant, at times funny story of Bernard Mednicki, a working-class, activist member of his socialist union in pre-Nazi Belgium who flees with his family to the mountainous region of southern France when the Nazis invade in 1940, assumes a Christian identity, and, through a series of street-smart moves, joins the Maquis, the French resistance.

> While there, he commits an act of self-preservation so horrendous, he represses it for over forty years. Only while working with internationally known book coach and editor Ken Wachsberger is he able to unleash the memory and find the peace he needs to join his ancestors.

Bernard is a storyteller supreme, in the best tradition of legendary Yiddish storytellers Chaim Potok, Bernard Malamud, and Isaac Bashevis Singer.

He wrote his story to preserve his legacy for his descendants. Bernard's subsequent life-transformation shows the power of writing as an instrument of healing.

I clicked the first bubble under Publishing Rights because Bernard and I own the copyright.

Keywords I left blank at first because the logical ones I wanted to use—Maquis, French resistance, Bernard Mednicki—already appeared in the description. Then I found inspiration and added "Volvic during World War II" and "Belgium during World War II" because those were Bernard's two primary homes in the story. In the same vein, I added "Russia during the pogroms" to capture Bernard's roots pre-Belgium. Then I added "writing for healing" and "writing to create a legacy" because those are the titles of talks I give as a book coach and speaker and Bernard's story is an example of both.

Keywords are the terms we use in online searches to find whatever we're trying to find. What keywords will your readers likely search to find your book? Keywords can be one word or a phrase.

I won't pretend to be an expert on choosing categories but you get to choose up to two from their drop-down list of options. I went with Nonfiction > Biography & Autobiography > Personal Memoirs; and Nonfiction > History > Holocaust. Convince me there are better alternatives; I'm open to change.

The last question on this page asked for an assessment of the Adult Content. No, I asserted, this book does not "contain language, situations, or images inappropriate for children under 18 years of age?" In this era of mass censorship and fear, I have no doubt others will disagree.

And that was it for the paperback details.

Paperback Content

On the Paperback Content page, I input my paperback ISBN. Remember, every other format you use—ebook, hardcopy, audiobook—requires its own ISBN. I was given the option of using a free ISBN from Kindle or my own. Please, use your own. You can read about ISBNs at "Get Your Own ISBN and Barcode."

I left publication date blank, so the default date became the date it went live on Amazon.

I always try to make my copyright dates meaningful. My copyright date was November 13, 2022, which was Bernard's birthday.

The print option I chose first was black and white interior with white paper, recommended for nonfiction. Cream paper is the recommended option for fiction. Then I looked closely: "and memoirs." I had already opted for memoir as one of my categories so I switched to cream paper.

Last three fields:

- Trim size: 6 x 9
- Bleed setting: no bleed
- Paperback cover finish: matte

Uploading Your Files

Next, you upload the manuscript and book cover files for your book.

If you followed the guidelines or hired a typesetter and graphic artist, your files will likely be approved, usually in a matter of hours, but you aren't ready to order books yet. Next step is to look at your book on screen through the previewer. If it looks good, approve it.

Then go back to your bookshelf and click the ellipsis ("…") on the right side of the book's entry. There, you can order up to five proof copies. Order at least one for your own careful final review. Within a few hours, Kindle sets up your proof copy and sends you an email to complete the purchase.

Pricing, Distribution, and Reviewing Your Proof Copy

Meanwhile, you are directed automatically to the pricing page. Here are the fields:

- Territories: Defaults to "All territories (worldwide rights)." Keep that one to make your book available all over the world.

- Primary marketplace: For U.S. readers this will be Amazon.com. Don't worry. Your book will be available at the other Amazon stores as well.

- Pricing, royalty, and distribution: All you have to fill in here is your desired list price. The converted prices for the other Amazon marketplaces will be automatically filled in. Yes, it's fun to receive royalties from non-U.S. markets.

You will notice the box that says "Expanded Distribution." Best advice I can give: Don't check it. The distribution promised by Amazon's Expanded Distribution can be obtained by IngramSpark, which bookstores much prefer over Amazon. D2D will get your book everywhere Amazon and IngramSpark can get it. After completing the pricing page, hit Save. Then wait for your proof copy to arrive in the mail, usually in a week give or take. Review it carefully.

If it looks good, go back online, approve your files, and wait for Kindle to do their final review, a process that takes a day or less, usually much less. Assuming your files are good, your book goes live online. If you just published a print version, order your first shipment for inventory.

Before you announce to your public, make sure your website and social media pages are finished.

Chapter 21

UPLOADING YOUR POD TO DRAFT2DIGITAL

The process of turning your electronic files into a book on Draft2Digital is similar to the process for Kindle, using mostly the same information.

But D2D offers the additional service of letting you design and typeset your Word file and cover, eliminating your need to farm out those services.

For Kindle, the files are expected to be camera-ready. D2D files are a work in progress.

My deepest appreciation goes out to Tara Robinett, Director of Operations at D2D, and others from D2D IT, who shared their wisdom and experience freely with me through tutorials, emails, and phone calls, and enabled me to write this guide.

Getting Started with Draft2Digital

To begin:

1. Set up Draft2Digital account and log in.

2. Press "My Books" button in top right-hand corner of page. On the next page, check "Add New Book."

3. On the next page, decide if you're going to do an ebook or print book and click the related button. You'll return to do the other one later. I clicked "Start Print Book" and was taken to the "Create New Print Book" page.

Create New Print Book

On the "Create New Print Book" page, you begin to provide the metadata that enables your readers to find you on the web; and D2D to automatically create your end matter pages and book cover, if you opt in to that D2D service.

The information you provide for one format is automatically applied to every format of your book, including softcover, hardcover, ebook, and audiobook, so you don't have to input the same information multiple times.

The Cover

To begin, you answer merely whether or not you have front cover art. If you say you don't, you're reminded that you can't publish until you do. If you say you do, a browse bar appears so you can upload your front cover art. If your file includes wraparound art for the spine and back cover, it doesn't work here.

Although I was happy with the cover I used on my Amazon version of *Never Be Afraid*, I was curious about how D2D's wraparound method would compare. I love the idea of this service. You give them a cover photo and cover text (front, back, and spine), and they'll create the back cover and spine by wrapping around a matching color scheme and the complete cover text. For free.

As Tara notes: "… many authors find [creating full-wraparound covers] to be a barrier to getting into print. They cannot afford to hire a cover designer to have one created for them, and our tool allows a great deal of customization just using the front cover image already available."

I said I had an image and uploaded my Amazon ebook cover file.

Everything Else

Next, they ask for your book title, publisher name, and author name. your book's serial number, and its volume number. The latter two fields didn't apply to me. I was surprised, though, that they didn't have a field for edition, which would have applied. That was, after all, my third edition of *Never Be Afraid.*

But, no, here's what IT told me: "There is no place to enter the edition number in our system. You can note this on your cover, or if you use your own copyright page in your file, you could also note it there."

- This is a flaw in the system that I encourage D2D to correct.

In the meantime, because my book was a revised edition, I had to opt out of their offer to automatically generate my title and copyright pages, and instead design my own. I included edition number on both pages.

The default language is English.

Search terms I used were the same as I used on Kindle, where they are called keywords:

- Volvic during World War II
- Belgium during World War II
- Russia during the pogroms
- writing for healing
- writing to create a legacy

I assured them that my book does not contain content inappropriate for minors.

The last field on that page, the BISACS (Book Industry Standards and Communications Subjects) code, is a drop-down list of subject headings and subheadings used by the publishing industry to help retailers, distributors, and librarians find your book. Imagine walking up and down the aisles of a bookstore and browsing the shelves. You can include up to five but, D2D advises, many of their vendors only support the first two so make them the most important. If you change your mind, you can move them around easily.

Kindle didn't have a BISACS field but they had a Categories field with the same drop-down menu. I used the same two: Nonfiction > Biography &

Autobiography > Personal Memoirs; and Nonfiction > History > Holocaust. Finally, I pressed "Start Print Book."

Print Book Details

After confirming that you understand their changes policy, you are taken to the "Print Book Details" page.

Just Getting Started

Here, at last, I uploaded my inside text file. But, unlike Kindle, where, as I noted earlier, my file must be camera-ready, here I'm just getting started. All you need to do is upload your manuscript as a Word file and D2D's system will let you format it for yourself (see "Preparing Your Manuscript File for Draft2Digital") using their broad selection of templates.

The default print book release date is the day you fill out the form. You obviously won't use it. Whatever date you pick, give yourself enough time so you can meet the deadline and not have to change the date.

The book description I took from Kindle and italicized the book title because I could.

On the bottom half of the page, you add the names of any "paid collaborators," which means co-authors.

Opt-In Section

This is followed by the opt-in section of boxes to check. They include introductory pages (Title, Copyright, Dedication), biographical pages (About the Author, About the Publisher), and promotional pages (Also By, New Release Email Notification Signup, Teaser),

You check the box if you want D2D to automatically generate the page based on other information you provide. It's a brilliant idea.

But not every page performs well under that formula.

For instance, because they didn't have an edition field, the program could not automatically indicate that my book was in its third edition. So, I had to opt out of Title and Copyright and upload my own title and copyright pages.

I could have skipped their Dedication box also because I was satisfied with my current page, which said simply, "To Bernard, who joined his ancestors and his two beloved wives on January 2, 1995." But I wanted to see what their version would look like so I opted in and checked it.

D2D can generate your About the Author page for the back of your book if you fill in your author information beforehand. I hadn't so I did, then checked About the Author. To learn more about Contributor Profiles, visit Account > Contributor Profiles.

I didn't have an About the Publisher page and didn't want one. I left that box unchecked.

I left Also By and Teaser unchecked because I haven't published any other books yet through D2D and I didn't want to omit my many other books, which were published through other distribution platforms.

When you check New Release Email Notifications Signup, D2D adds a page that enables readers to be notified of any new books you publish. With ebooks, you can't check it if you are a co-author, which I am, so I didn't check it for print either for consistency.

Use Your Own ISBN

I used my own ISBN, as you should do also.

Finally, I hit "Save & Continue."

This was the first time I was able to "Save and Continue," another flaw, I believe, in the system that is easily rectified. At Amazon, you can just hit Save any time you log off. The next time you log on, you will be taken to your book page where you can "continue setup" of your new book and be taken to where you left off.

Print Book Inside

On the Print Book Inside page, you choose your paper color, the trim size, and whether or not you want your table of contents automatically generated.

Where the Magic Takes Place

The Print Book Inside page is the most fun of the set-up pages because here is where the magic takes place. You begin with D2D's wide selection of template styles for your book's interior design, which they have placed in the following categories: All-Purpose, Mystery and Thriller, Romance, Science Fiction and Fantasy, Non-Fiction, and Poetry.

Plan to spend some time perusing the styles and seeing what they do with drop-caps, chapter titles, paragraphing, and scene breaks. I went with D2D Block, one of the nonfiction templates.

I loved it because it was airier than my Word file version, which made the text easier to read. Of course, the negative side of that positive is that the airiness added pages, which increased the unit cost of books.

You also determine placement for your page numbers and header text.

Page Numbering

Getting your page numbering to begin where you want it to begin is easy once your text outline is correct and produces a TOC that D2D's program can pick up (see "Preparing Your Manuscript File for Draft2Digital"). I started mine with the introduction, after the front matter.

Traditional page numbering uses Roman numerals for front matter and Arabic numbers for the main text. D2D at present does not offer the capability of using Roman numerals so, I was advised, if I wanted Roman numerals, I would have to create my own pdf. I decided to go without Roman numerals.

- Suggestion to D2D: Include Roman numeral capability.

Table of Contents

But the only way for chapter titles to show up in the table of contents was to make the chapter number and the chapter title both Heading 1's. When I did that, the numbers and titles showed up fine, even appearing in their entirety over more than one line. But the design looked amateurish.

- Suggestion to D2D: Include a Heading 2 for chapter title in the program so titles can be formatted separately from chapter numbers.
- Bonus suggestion to D2D: Include a Heading 3 for brief chapter blurbs to enhance the table of contents.

I continued to opt in with D2D's TOC because I liked that they are able to automatically identify on what page each chapter begins and fill the table of contents with those pages.

But when I inspected the automatically generated pdf, I discovered the table of contents staring at me from where the title page should have been. When you opt in on the table of contents but not the title and copyright pages, the table of contents gets programmatically placed ahead of them. To get the front matter to appear in the traditional order, I was told, I would have to upload my own pdf.

- Suggestion to D2D: Enhance the program to include a place setter for each front matter page so that the title page always comes up first no matter who supplies it, and so on with the other pages.

I had two other issues as well with the automatically generated program:

- I couldn't eliminate the subtitle in the page header.
- On two blank pages, for some reason, the header showed up when it was unwanted.

That was as far as I could go. I knew I needed Cal to give me my own custom pdf to upload.

But I loved the D2D Block template. Its airiness was easy on the eyes, and the default setting for widows and orphans produced a manuscript with none of either! Cal's rendition preserved the airiness of D2D Block but with a different typeface, also had no widows and orphans, and got rid of those unwanted headers.

Print Book Cover

Next you come to the Print Book Cover page. You've already uploaded the file. Now you add the details to create your wraparound cover.

Cover Finish

For cover finish, you can go with matte or glossy. When I published my first book, *Beercans on the Side of the Road: The Story of Henry the Hitchhiker*, I went with the glossy cover because I thought it looked more attractive. Never again. The covers could barely stay scuff free in a crosstown car ride; and shrink wrap was a luxury I couldn't afford.

Spine

The default spine text had author names on the upper spine and book title on the lower spine. I reversed them with cut and paste, then uploaded my Azenphony Press logo. If I wanted, which I didn't, I could have deleted the subtitle.

Back Cover

Fields for Print Cover Description and Back Cover Biography give the program back-cover text. My bio fit the allowed space. Then I added two testimonial quotes into the description field because there was no field for Testimonial Quotes. Unfortunately, the quotes pushed my description text over my space quota. I added them instead to the beginning of my bio where they fit fine after I cut one sentence from my bio.

- Suggestion to D2D: Add a Testimonial Quotes field. Quotes are a vital back-cover marketing tool.

You've Got the Time

I opted out of a back-cover photo.

The final result for the back cover showed way too much blank space until I adjusted the type size. The revised text looked as good as my Amazon cover but I wanted to replace the Times New Roman typeface with Calibri because Calibri is friendlier to the eyes of the sight-impaired.

Unfortunately, Calibri isn't an option. Fortunately, Roboto bears a close resemblance to Calibri and is. I went with it.

The solid brown background lacked the nuance of my original but, I was pleased to note, sharpened the white text so it was more easily readable.

If you like your own version better, by all means use it instead. If you do, though, be sure to include the blank space on the back lower right-hand corner where the barcode will be automatically added.

I kept the D2D version.

Print Book Price

After applying changes, saving, and continuing, you get to the Print Book Price page. Here you

- select your sale price (and learn immediately what your sale price and royalty will be for each book sold in Australia, Canada, Europe, and Great Britain);
- declare your level of rights ownership (original creator, have secured rights, public domain); and
- confirm that you have read D2D's terms of service and understand that, once you publish, you may make changes to the cover and text only once every ninety days.

When you save, you are immediately warned that, if you use your own ISBN, you can't reuse it with Amazon "should you decide to go direct to KDP Print in the future."

Print Book Approve

You're so close now, you can just about smell the printed pages.

On this page, you are given two choices: to approve the pages that you have so far viewed only electronically; or to order a physical proof copy.

Best advice: Always order the proof copy. Maybe not often but sometimes errors that don't show up on screen jump out at you in print.

I was advised that I would be paying $30 for the proof copy to be printed priority and expedited to me. I hoped, when I got to my shopping cart, I would discover they were merely offering a suggestion that I could reject. At Amazon, the cost of a proof copy is the same as the price of an author copy and delivery time with non-expedited service has usually been about a week.

Unfortunately, they weren't. I paid the $30 plus $1.80 sales tax. In their defense, Amazon has the economy-of-scale advantage.

Eight days later, my proof copy arrived. I opened it with trepidation as I anticipated any number of possible negative outcomes but I found none. So, after several hours of looking for reasons why my immediate impression was flawed and the file was not ready, I returned to the Approve page and approved the proof copy for publication and distribution.

I submitted my answers.

"Print Book Success!" I was informed instantly. I had been impressed with Kindle's review in up to a day. I ordered a first run of fifty and then uploaded my ebook.

The Link to Everywhere

As soon as your ebook is successfully received, your Universal Book Link (UBL) is created automatically on My Books. The UBL is one link that leads to all formats of your book at all vendors that are part of D2D's distribution network. It is a gift from D2D to help you inform your readers where your book is available and in what format.

You can customize your UBL to make it memorable. For instance, I changed mine from books2read.com/u/bQNXke to books2read.com/neverbeafraid.

But here's the caveat: It only automatically picks up stores that sell your ebook. As Jamie in IT explained, "Print book links are wired differently, and will never be recognized automatically."

The good news is, they can be added manually:

> To add a Print Link, log in to your Books2Read.com account; then click on LINK TOOLS and slide down to select UBL Dashboard. Next, click on the book title you'd like to add print links to. Expand the Print section by clicking on the yellow "Print Links" or the plus sign. Click on the icon of the store you want to add a link to and a store-specific link input will show up above the icons.

> Paste your store link into the input and be sure to select the type of book it is: paperback, hardcover, or large-print. Lock in to save your link!

> The full link directly from the vendor's listing page should be used; no short links are supported.

Your challenge is to find the right store-specific link. As Eda, also from IT, expands:

> In order to find the print URLs, I'm afraid you will need to search the Internet to find which stores are carrying your print book. Unfortunately, we do not provide these links; each channel partner makes the decision whether to make a title available and how to display the availability of a title.

* * *

In judging Draft2Digital's program overall, I found their plan to be brilliant and promising. The templates, table of contents, wraparound covers, extended distribution network, and Universal Book Links are gifts to authors. Their dashboard is the most user-friendly digital book dashboard I've ever seen. IT service members are responsive and friendly.

They need to finish the job, beginning with my simple suggestions. And cut back on the ninety-day waiting period between allowable edits.

A good PR idea: Ask users for their suggestions and actively add the best ones

Chapter 22

PREPARING YOUR MANUSCRIPT FILE FOR DRAFT2DIGITAL

Whereas the files you submit to Kindle have to be camera-ready, for D2D you can submit only a Word file of your main text. That's it, but be consistent in your outline format so their program can pick up the pattern and reformat it.

For instance, center all chapter titles in

BOLD ALL CAPS

Do the same for front matter and back matter titles:

INTRODUCTION

Headings within chapters can be centered and bold also but capitalizing only

First Letter of First Word and Main Words

Subheadings can be

Flush Left Bold

I end chapters and end matter sections with Insert > Page Break just because I want to. But, in fact, that extra safeguard isn't necessary because the system is already programmed to turn your next Header 1 into a new title.

When you fill out the requested fields, they are able to automatically construct the front matter and back matter (collectively called end matter) for you. This is a wonderful service.

However, you need to review what they give you for each page and decide if you are satisfied with it. If not, you'll want to opt out of that service for that page and provide your own. (I explain more about opting in and out in "Uploading Your POD to Draft2Digital").

Chapter 23

PRESERVING REVIEWS
IN SUBSEQUENT EDITIONS ON AMAZON

I wrote in the first edition of *You've Got the Time* that, when you publish a second edition on Amazon and obtain the required new ISBN, you lose the reviews you got from the first edition. The solution, I said, was to call it a second printing of the first edition, keep the current ISBN, and preserve the reviews.

Let Me Try That Again

You can forget that advice. Even after your first edition is officially out of print, you can link the reviews from earlier editions to the book page of later editions. That's why you're reading this second edition of *You've Got the Time*.

As Jonatan in Kindle IT told me, "If the first version of your book was uploaded on KDP and the second one as well, we can take both ASIN numbers, unify them in our systems, and the reviews are transferred. If you use KDP to publish one version of the book and another publishing medium to publish the second version and only Amazon as the selling site, we cannot take the ASIN number to unify them, because that second version is not part of your KDP account."

The ASIN number is what Amazon uses to keep track of ebook sales.

Daniela, another IT expert, added: "If we link both versions, the old version has to be unpublished so we can manually link ... the customer reviews from the old version to the new version of your book."

In other words, Kindle IT couldn't get to my Kindle dashboard through D2D even though Amazon is part of D2D's distribution network. I had to publish two identical versions of this second edition. The solution, I thought, was easy. I just had to opt out of D2D softcover distribution on Amazon and upload directly from Kindle.

Print Exception

But, according to a contentious (on my part) clause in the contractual agreement between D2D and Ingram, authors are forbidden from opting out of Amazon or any other vendors, for print only. It's all or none.

With ebooks, D2D allows authors to opt in and out of each distribution network as they choose. Why the difference with softcovers?

As Jamie in IT explained:

> I understand that you purchased your own ISBNs with the intentions of using one per book, but you have to see our point that when you use the same number and publish direct with Amazon, then again with D2D, the waters become muddied. If there is a problem with the book showing improperly, no cover, description is wrong (these things do happen) how will you know who to report the issue to? Amazon will say, it's not our fault, talk to D2D. D2D would never say that, but we would have to spend man hours investigating if it is indeed our listing with the problem, and what to do about it. Dealing with vendors is very time consuming and can be frustrating.

I wondered if authors could safely ignore the mandate.

According to Jamie, it's a crapshoot:

> I see posts daily on social media about how authors can publish their print books using the same ISBN if they hit the publish button very quickly at the same time on two sites. I feel bad because I have seen, from the back side of things, that problems can happen, and everything is fine and rosy until it isn't one day, then sorting out two books with the same ISBN on 2 distributor sites will be a headache

for the author as well as a small company like D2D…. Some books get through using the same ISBN. People try it all the time. The ones that don't get through (and we can never tell if they will or if they won't) are in for a struggle to get published, and the author usually has to delist and start over with a new ISBN.

The only solution they would accept required authors to get a second ISBN for the identical D2D softcover edition.

Resolution

I quivered. Current industry practice says each format has its own ISBN and it may be used across sales platforms. The D2D-Ingram agreement threatened to make ISBN platform-dependent. I wasn't comfortable being a part of that deviation from tradition.

Instead, I proposed, I would continue my upload to D2D using the same ISBN as the softcover that's already on Amazon and then unpublish my Amazon edition and allow D2D to handle my Amazon distribution.

They said to give it a try.

My route to resolution was roundabout because I was figuring out how to deal with the idiosyncrasies of both Amazon and D2D for the first time while my softcover was already on Amazon. You can save time and *tsouris* (Yiddish for "pain in the butt") by following these simple steps:

- Upload your revised ebook file to Kindle to distribute on Amazon.
- Follow below instructions to preserve reviews from earlier edition.
- Upload same ebook file to D2D to distribute everywhere in network except Amazon.
- Upload softcover file to D2D for distribution throughout network.

How to Transfer Your Reviews to the Next Edition

The transfer itself is easy. Here's what you do:

1. On your bookshelf, go to the current edition of your book the one that will soon be obsolete, click the ellipsis and unpublish.

2. Next, you have to give Kindle that edition's all-important Amazon Standard Identification Number (ASIN), the ten- digit code that Amazon uses to keep track of its inventory. Unfortunately, you can't reach them on the home Contact U page. Here's what you can do:

    *   On the home Contact Us page, click Amazon Store & Product Detail Page and then link to "Link your print and Kindle editions." I thought linking formats of the same edition might lead me to "Link two editions" but that information does not exist on their website, a fixable flaw in their system that affects nonfiction writers, especially academics, more than fiction writers.

    *   Fortunately, on that same page, they offer two ways to connect with them:

        a. A "Call us" button that will connect you with a real person. I spoke with Zaahid, who was courteous and helpful.

        b. A yellow "Start chat" button that begins your live chat. Zaahid suggested I advise authors to use this method. Simply type in your ASIN and, Zaahid assures me, they will take it from there.

3. The transfer of reviews takes between two and seven business days. Watch your site. If the connection hasn't shown up by that time, contact them again.

Chapter 24

GRAB YOUR SHARE OF THE GROWING
AUDIOBOOK MARKET

You've come this far in the publishing process and created print and electronic versions of your book. Why stop now? Turn your book into an audiobook. Grab your share of the growing audience of book lovers who would love to listen to your book while they're running errands in the car, while they're walking in the park, while they're riding the stationary bike at the gym, and while they're drifting off to sleep.

According to David Wolf, founder of audiobook production company Audivita Studios, the audiobook market has been growing at an annual rate exceeding 22% since 2015. Eighty thousand new audiobook titles enter the $2.5 billion market every year. "There is a growing perceived or actual 'scarcity' of time people feel they can spend sitting and reading, which presents an opportunity for authors across the spectrum."

If these book lovers want to listen to their books, your book will never make it into their libraries — unless you turn it into an audiobook.

Finding Your Voice (or Someone Else's)

The first question to ask yourself, Wolf says, is, "Who will narrate the text?" Sometimes the author knows who the narrator will be going into the first conversation with the production company. At other times, that decision is made in the initial consultation.

> The answer is generally strategic, or based on the capacity of the author to actually perform the reading, which is not as easy as it seems. If there is a clear business case for the author to be the "voice" in the

audiobook, then I recommend we go that direction for production. If they don't have the time or the ability to do the recording, and/or if it's not critical that *they* are the voice, then we'll do casting calls and hire a professional voice actor to do it.

Setting Up Your Schedule

Once the method of determining a narrator has been decided, the company provides a quote for services and begins scheduling the following steps:

- Recording: Done in-person or remotely using an HD recording platform that runs native on the Google Chrome browser. Sessions are generally limited to not more than two hours at one time.
- Post-production: Includes all editing; removal of outtakes, retakes, and unwanted audio; and applying noise reduction, equalization, and audio compression.
- Final audio mastering process: Ensuring that the technical specifications comply with the requirements of Audible, Amazon, and Apple iTunes.
- Create the square cover graphic: Recommended size: 2400 x 2400 pixels and 72 dots per inch (dpi).
- Uploading: We'll get to this in a minute.

The entire process takes an estimated four to eight weeks, depending on the length of the audiobook. "The quality control approval process at Audible, Amazon, and iTunes usually takes, collectively, an additional two to three weeks, after which the audiobook goes live immediately."

Going It Alone

How much of the job can reasonably be done DIY?

Looking at the author-read scenario, the answer "depends on the skillset of the author, the resources, the equipment, and the recording setup available to them."

Most authors are not really equipped to handle the entire process themselves because of the audio post-production standards and specs. That said, I have worked with authors who have a high-quality microphone, a platform to record themselves doing the raw (source) recordings, and the ability to "self-produce" their own performance.

In these cases, we set up a Dropbox folder for the project and the author DIY's the recordings (with some consultation from us). Then we take it from there with the full editing, post-production portion, and file management/uploading to the retail platform.

Recommended technology for the author-read scenario:

• the Samson Q2U USB/XLR Dynamic Microphone (under $100)

• a set of headphones or ear buds so authors can hear themselves in the headset while performing and take remote directions

For audio recording, he recommends software such as Audacity that is available for free online.

How Much Does Audio Publishing Cost?

Pricing strategies may differ among audio service providers. At Audivita, the quoted budget for the author-read option is $.10 per word. So, a 50,000-word book would cost $5,000 to produce, turnkey, including setting up the audiobook for online retail distribution.

Typically, narrator cost can range from $100 to $350 per finished hour of audio. The final finished running time for a 50,000-word book will be about 5.5 hours. Many professional narrators include the editing and post production in that cost.

If they don't include the editing and post production, that can take 32 hours at a studio hourly rate range of $50 to $100.

So, for a 50,000-word book, a ballpark total cost estimate might be $4,000 to $6,000, depending in part on whether Audivita casts talent or records the author remotely.

To help contain costs, they often hire talent on a "royalty-only" basis. "We price these projects on a flat-rate basis ranging from $350 to $500 per audiobook, sometimes more depending on the requirements."

Additional costs may find their way into projects that require multiple voice actors or that employ well-known celebrities or high-priced voice actors.

Bells and whistles?

- Amazon/Audible offers a product called "Whisper Sync" for any title where the audio matches 97% of the ebook content. With Whisper Sync, consumers can switch between the ebook and audiobook versions while maintaining sync as they switch between the two formats.
- "In some cases, we might provide music cues or sound design to augment the audiobook, but this is rare, at least from our experience. We have provided musical-themed lead-ins at the chapter beginnings, which can be a nice touch."

Uploading Your Files

When the final audio and cover files are ready, upload them to the desired retail distribution platform and provide all the metadata. You can select from over thirty retail distribution channels that support Audible, Amazon, and iTunes. With each one that you use, you'll want to set up an account for your audiobook like you did for your POD and ebook on Draft2Digital, Kindle, and IngramSpark.

Among the most popular platforms:

ACX

ACX is generally seen as the hub for Audible, Amazon, and iTunes. The decision whether or not to sign their exclusive agreement, Wolf believes, is a personal choice based on your distribution preferences and business strategy. With their exclusive deal, you get distributed only on Audible, Amazon, and iTunes and only through ACX. You can't use any other platform. Without the agreement, you still get onto Audible, Amazon, and iTunes, but you can explore other platforms as well.

The incentive to go exclusive? You get a bigger royalty: 40% of net sales versus 25% with the nonexclusive deal.

Findaway Voices

On July 17, 2017, Findaway Voices announced a partnership with Draft2Digital. If you produce your ebook through Draft2Digital, a click of a box at various points in the production process can send your files to Findaway. There, they can produce your audiobook and distribute it at over forty major audiobook retailers and library partners, including Amazon, Apple, Scribd, Audible, Google Play, Kobo, Barnes and Noble, Baker & Taylor, and Spotify. Their combined network reaches listeners in more than 170 countries.

As an author and publisher, you keep complete control over content, pricing, and distribution. You connect with professional narrators, are guided through production, and are provided with a high-quality audiobook. You can upload your files for free.

Findaway pays 80% of net sales and is nonexclusive. You can use Findaway Voices and ACX both as long as you aren't exclusive with ACX.

According to Findaway's website:

> An average audiobook created with Findaway Voices has about 50,000 words and costs between $1,000 and $2,000. We can estimate the cost of your audiobook by multiplying a per-finished-hour narrator rate with the estimated length of your finished recording. The longer the book, the higher the estimate will be.

But Findaway doesn't have to be your producer to get your audiobook into their network. You can produce your audiobook elsewhere, then skip production services at Findaway and go straight to Findaway's distribution platform.

Authors' Republic

Authors' Republic's website isn't nearly as personable as Findaway's and they pay 10% less in royalties, but 70% is still way better, and with a nonexclusive agreement, than ACX pays with an exclusive agreement; and they get your audiobook into over thirty channels.

Always

No matter which platforms you use, you can also sell directly from your website. Unless you sign an exclusive agreement.

Charging for Your Audiobook

Although you can charge whatever you want while selling your audiobook through your own private channels, "Each retailer of your audiobook independently prices your product and determines such price in their sole discretion."

Pricing on Audible, for instance, is generally based on audiobook length and ranges from $7 for under an hour to $25 to $35 for over 20 hours.

Selecting an Audiobook Company

In selecting an audiobook company, look for referrals from other authors. Call the company to ask questions. Make sure you have a comfort level and confidence with the process, the people, and the budget.

Seek to do as much of the process yourself as you are inclined and can afford, both in time and in money. Narrating is your most logical role.

But don't nickel-dime. Professional services are out there. You don't want your independently produced audiobook to look independently produced. If you're like most authors, you don't have the time, bandwidth, or audio production expertise to perform the recording, the editing, and post-production. Consider farming out as much of the work as you can so you can get to work where you're needed: promoting and selling copies of your book in all of its versions.

Remember: An audiobook requires its own ISBN.

PART 5: PROMOTING AND SELLING YOUR BOOK

Chapter 25

BUILD YOUR INCOME STREAM

Writing and publishing your book is the easy part. Promoting and selling it is where the hard work begins. That's also where dollars are spent and earned and your reputation is established.

Embrace the Process

So, embrace the process. Have fun with it. You have more ways to market and move books than you will ever have time to implement and more ways to measure success than just book sales.

As an author, you can take trips you never would have dreamed of taking without your book. You can be quoted and appear in every form of media "already invented or yet to be invented" (to steal a quote from traditional book contracts).

I travelled to conferences all over the country to speak with like-minded souls, students, long-time friends, and potential readers about my adventures in the Vietnam-era antiwar movement thanks to my four-volume Voices from the Underground Series about the independent, antiwar underground press.

Sometimes I was paid for speaking. At others, I spoke for free but got reimbursed for travel, food, and lodging expenses. I always sold books. Whenever I could, I arranged to have my talk videoed so I could upload it to YouTube and my website.

Sometimes I initiated the outreach to conference organizers and asked to speak. At others, they came to me.

It'll be the same for you. Who is your audience? What conferences do they attend? Make your availability to speak known.

And you can write off expenses on your annual taxes: for travel, for food, for your phone, for supplies and equipment, for research and education, for web maintenance, charitable contributions, promotion, and so much more. Your accountant is the last word on what you can write off, not me, but if you make purchases in any of those categories, save your receipts and begin developing your case for how they relate to your business and should be deductible.

Build Your Income Stream

The keyword to publication success is "income stream." Book sales may be a significant part of your income stream, especially when you publish in hard cover, soft cover, ebook, and audio.

But don't stop there. As a thought leader in your specialty area, you can teach college classes, lead workshops, sell courses online, host webinars and speak in front of major conferences.

You can negotiate with conference organizers to purchase copies of your book to stuff in gift bags when you're delivering the keynote speech.

Sometimes your book is a source of income. At other times, you give away books to attract a related but greater source of income. At tax time, you can usually write off the cost to purchase most books you give away.

To promote your book and your expertise, you can write articles on your blog and link to other sites or get them to link to yours. You can use the articles to create chapters of new books. You can link to them from whatever social media you use.

No one next step is correct for every promotional campaign. Just keep moving. The more steps you take, the easier it becomes to take the next step.

You've Got the Time

Two Proud Professions

One lesson I've learned: As an author, you need to be a speaker, too, if you want to make significant money from your books.

Join the National Speakers Association to learn the business of speaking and discover an amazing network of contacts, mentors, and friends. Become active with Toastmasters to learn the skill and craft of public speaking.

At the same time, join the National Writers Union, where you will learn about the world of freelance writing and publishing, ask questions, and share your own sage wisdom on NWU-BOOK, NWU's active listserv for book authors. In addition, if you find yourself looking at a book contract, you can request the free services of a trained book contract adviser — worth well more than the cost of membership alone.

You aren't a writer who speaks or a speaker who writes. You are a writer and a speaker, a member of two proud professions that work together. Become knowledgeable about both worlds and how they come together.

I'm grateful to the generosity of the book promoters, coaches, web designers, and social media experts who have shared their marketing wisdom and experiences in the following pages. In the back of the book, in "Further Resources," I refer you to books — many by these same experts — and other sources that will push your publishing and marketing adventure way beyond the limits of where I can take you.

The world of book marketing is so vast, no one book can cover it all. I suggest a few others in "Further Resources."

Chapter 26

IT STARTS WITH A BUSINESS PLAN

You can make a lot of money with your book if you don't get overwhelmed with the vast amount of marketing options. Bestselling author David Dye, president of Let's Grow Leaders, encourages writers to develop a business plan, which includes your marketing plan:

> The most common mistake I see is that authors start writing without a plan. If you're writing to explore your thoughts, that's good. If you're writing to sell your work, you want to think through your ideal buyer and reader.

"Know Your Jennifer"

How do you find your ideal buyer and reader? "Know your Jennifer."

> The idea behind "Know your Jennifer" is that you pick a specific person who embodies your ideal reader and then write to them. Create a list of their goals and their problems. Use these key desires to construct your outline.

Then build your platform, build your marketing plan, and use them to inform your writing and the book's design. "Whether it's people who follow you online, subscribers, fans, or some other tribe, the bigger your tribe and the more relevant the book is to them, the more you'll sell."

And don't delay in starting your promotion, the second most common mistake of authors. Marketing Hall of Famer Seth Godin, he notes, says to start promoting three years before you publish.

That means you're building your platform, sharing your ideas, and gathering a tribe. Connect with other authors and influencers and promote their work; share their work generously long before you ask them to share and promote yours.

Elements of a Sample Business Plan Outline

Writing your business plan, Dye notes, helps you to identify your market and learn who else is competing for that same market. It helps you discover ways to stand out from them.

> In addition to identifying your key buyer, reader, platform, and marketing plan, do the research around similar titles. What will your work say that adds to the discussion? Either that differs with conventional wisdom or extends it? How does your book figure into your larger business ecosystem, if you have one? Is it a credibility builder? A platform to sell keynote speaking and training or coaching? Or maybe you're using it to sell other resources like a workbook?

Here is a sample business plan outline for Dye's *Winning Well: A Manager's Guide to Getting Results — Without Losing Your Soul*. You can easily adapt it to your book:

- Testimonials: Compile testimonial quotes and videos from book readers, conference attendees, clients, and anyone else who benefited from your words and actions (see "Tracking Down Experts for Forewords and Testimonial Quotes"). In addition to including them in your plan, you can publish them in your book and post them on your website.

- Executive summary: An overview of the complete document so someone reading just this part can get a good feel for the rest. What will readers get from your book? How will it help them?"

- Summary of the book: Include not only a summary of the main text but your anticipated page length and number of chapters. If you're writing a proposal, this section will give them a feel for your writing. It is an energetic, attention-grabbing introduction to the topic that sets the stage and then walks them through what they'll get in this book.

- The market: Who is your ideal reader? Who cares about your book enough to buy copies or hear you speak? Where will you be able to round up some quantity sales? Who is your competition?

- The author: Why are you qualified to write this book? What have you accomplished that gives you credibility?

- Author's platform and marketing plan: Include social media networks you frequent, email strategy, personal appearances and speeches, public relations plans, strategy for free and paid ads, and any other ways that will help you sell books. Which services will you purchase? Which can you handle yourself?

- Book outline and sample chapters: These elements are most important if you're preparing a package to send to a prospective publisher. Title your chapters with benefit statements that your ideal reader will find irresistible. For example, Dye's *Winning Well*, a book he wrote for managers, includes a chapter named "How to Run Meetings That Get Results and People Want to Attend."

"You can leverage relationships with other influencers, authors, bloggers, and podcasters if you've built those relationships and been generous with them," he says. "When it comes time to promote, find ways for your network to win with you. Promote them as they promote you."

He is especially fond of the blog as a marketing tool:

The first use of the blog is to explore ideas that will go in the book and to build a following of people who are interested in those ideas. These are likely future buyers and promoters. When it comes time to launch your book, don't just ask your tribe to buy — engage them to promote it. Have fun, get creative — you can run contests, get social

189

media photos, do buy one/give one promotions. Your imagination is the limit.

Do I Need a Publicist?

Finally, understand the role of publicity and the publicist. Dye reminds authors that publicity doesn't sell books. It sells you and builds your credibility.

Look for publicists with proven track records and clients who you can talk with about their experience. As you think about PR, focus on where your readers are most likely to see or hear you: print, online articles, radio, podcasts, television. Ideally, find publicists who will train you to take best advantage of the opportunities they provide. You want to use those articles and interviews as effectively as you can.

Chapter 27

THINK LIKE A BESTSELLER – WHETHER OR NOT YOUR BOOK MAKES A LIST

Do you think being able to claim bestseller status for your book would boost sales and increase your credibility as an expert in your field?

David Newman: 39 Straight Months

It didn't hurt marketing expert, author, and speaker David Newman. For 39 straight months after its release in 2013, Newman rode the crest of bestseller status with his nonfiction business book, *Do It! Marketing: 77 Instant-Action Ideas to Boost Sales, Maximize Profits, and Crush Your Competition*. During the launch period alone, his book was, according to Amazon.com rankings:

- #1 Bestseller in Marketing for Small Business
- #2 Bestseller in Marketing
- #2 Bestseller in Entrepreneurship
- #1 in "Hot New Releases" in Marketing
- #2 in "Hot New Releases" in Marketing & Sales
- #2 Bestseller in Marketing (Paid Kindle Store)
- #2 in "Hot New Releases" in Marketing (Paid Kindle Store)
- #2 in "Hot New Releases" in Marketing for Small Business (Audible Audio Edition)

After the launch, his book never dropped below 20,000 sales rank of all 8 million+ books sold on Amazon for 39 months continuously, putting the book, according to Newman, "in the top quarter of one percent of ALL books sold, including Harry Potter and the Bible."

The Secret to Bestseller Success

His secret?

> Shameless, relentless, and continual promotion and cross-promotion with other experts via email marketing, social media, live events, podcast, and borrowing others' platforms via guest blogging and guest podcasts, asking for reviews at every opportunity, and in a few cases buying into some highly targeted email-based advertising that was a perfect fit with my target readership and was cost-effective.

"It's a self-reinforcing loop," he continues. "Readers want to know your book is popular and successful. The moment you start to gain some traction — media coverage, reviews, social posts, etc. — SPREAD and AMPLIFY that, so it builds on itself. Being shy never helped any author build their platform."

An essential tool for that effort, he offers, is your book's website presence:

> Many authors create one "book" page on their website and give a skimpy overview and a sample chapter download. That is no way enough. On my website, at the time of promoting my book, I had FIVE dedicated pages:
>
> 1. The Book
> 2. Book Bonuses
> 3. Book Preview (which included a video book trailer)
> 4. Bulk Orders (very important to give incentives and encourage bulk purchases)
> 5. Book Club (which also included a free Facebook community for readers to connect with each other and share ideas)

Embrace Your YOU Marketing Campaign

Finally, he advises, remember, your book is more than just a book. It as an integral part of your business:

The book needs to support the business — just as the business needs to pivot and support the book! All the things you should be and could be doing to promote your BOOK are probably the exact same things you should be doing ALL the time to promote your business in a healthy, vigorous, and ongoing way.

Don't think of it as a book marketing campaign; think of it as a YOU marketing campaign with the main distribution channel being your book!

Jeffrey Hayzlett: Leverage Your Content

Jeffrey Hayzlett sold thousands of books during a six-month-long kickoff campaign leading up to launch for his book, *Running the Gauntlet*. As a result, on day one the book was already a bestseller. The National Speakers Association's Hall of Fame member and author of *The Hero Factor: How Great Leaders Transform Organizations and Create Winning Cultures* (2019) did it by leveraging the content of the book to generate constant copy.

Typically, you have about two weeks to promote the book and, after that period, even your mother is sick of hearing about it. What I try to do is extend it past that two-week period–you need to have ears, eyeballs, hearts, and minds to be considered for sales. You also need to come up with content and ways to utilize that content.

How to Leverage Content

Here's what he did:

For example, I did a regular two weeks of promo, radio tour, media tour, and a few key book signings at Barnes & Noble on Fifth Ave, airport promos, and the kickoff and the beginning of the month. I decided to make every chapter title 140 characters or less to fit Twitter's requirements at that time, which gave me about 33 tweets, one for each chapter. The first 1,500 words of each chapter were turned into blog posts, which gave me 33 more days of activation.

Then I wrote a short blog post of about 250 to 500 words for each chapter, which gave me 33 additional activations. I also included a two-dimensional, branded barcode that I got through a vendor/client friend of mine, where people could text me; that led me to create a video for every chapter to talk about what they'd see in every chapter–a total of 119 extra days of activation.

Placing High on Amazon

To place high on Amazon's list, he had to register bulk orders strategically, not only on Amazon but on smaller retailers as well to increase distribution. Why? Because a bulk order of 500 books counts as one sale if you order them at the same time, and large orders create suspicion on the part of Amazon's algorithm monitors.

We went out to our friends, past customers, 30 to 100 different groups that buy books in bulk — organizations, promotional companies, whatever I could find — and I got them to give me their credit cards. Rather than place an entire order, I would start placing orders the day before launch, in increments, until I fulfilled all orders. About 100 books a day on Amazon will move you to bestseller.

Making Money by Giving Away Books

And yet sometimes the best financial reward comes from giving a book away: "When a person receiving the book is a potential customer and the value of giving it to them is greater than the cost of the book, that's when you give them away. You have to find the value in everything you do when it comes to getting your book out."

Planning for Hayzlett's promotion campaigns begins at least a year ahead of publication. "We look at objectives, press releases, media outreach, collateral materials, social activation, and every other component needed to surround the book launch. If you're not starting months in advance, you're already behind."

Kristi Lynn Davis: The Art of Choosing Your Categories

Okay, you're thinking, David Newman and Jeffrey Hayzlett are professional marketers. No wonder they did so well with their marketing. But you're not a marketing professional. You're a first-time author. Does being on the bestseller charts seem out of reach for you?

Bestseller First Time Out

It didn't for Kristi Lynn Davis. Davis is an entertainer, author, and transformation coach whose first book, *Long Legs and Tall Tales: A Showgirl's Wacky, Sexy Journey to the Playboy Mansion and the Radio City Rockettes,* made it, on the Amazon Bestseller list on launch day, to:

- #3 as a Kindle ebook in the category of Arts & Photography: Theater: Broadway & Musicals
- #8 in Books: Biographies & Memoirs: Arts & Literature: Theatre
- #11 in Books: Arts & Photography: Performing Arts: Theatre: Broadway & Musicals

"Which leads me to another important point," she notes. "Choosing which categories to put your book under also influences whether or not you will reach bestseller status. That is an art in and of itself."

She's been on and off the Amazon bestseller list (top 100) since she launched in 2015.

> I launched a bestseller campaign using Teresa De Grosbois's course as a guideline. Basically, you get as many people as you can to buy your book on the same day. But there were many, many steps to the process.

A Worthwhile Effort

Was the result worth the effort? For Kristi Lynn Davis it was.

Anyone can self-publish a book these days, but getting your book on an Amazon bestseller list carries some weight and demonstrates that you've already reached a certain level of success (even if it is only for one day in some obscure category); and that may inspire confidence in others to purchase your book or hire you to speak. But it won't necessarily make you rich. You've got to keep marketing your book as much as possible even after you hit the bestseller list.

Finally, writing her book transformed her life:

My life had many ups and downs and twists and turns during the fourteen years it took me to write my book. Several times I gave up writing altogether. So, the fact that I finally committed to the book and deemed it worthy of completing was truly transformative. My story was worth telling, and I believed in it. Then when people started purchasing it, reading it, and loving it, it was thrilling! I'm honored when my book can entertain and inspire others.

But running a bestseller campaign is a TON of work. It takes a lot of planning ahead. Take a course or read a book on how to do it because it is a complicated, tedious process. Start building fans TODAY by blogging and/or speaking. Start building your email list TODAY, because that will help you get the word out when you need your fans to buy your book on a specific day.

My Takeaways

Bottom line: Being known as a bestselling author has its perks but you've got to put in the work and not get lost in the adoration. Make it part of your business plan — but not your whole plan:

1. Build your fan base.
2. Create continuous content.
3. Escape the hype.
4. Develop your business plan.
5. Enjoy your status as a "bestselling author" forever.

You've Got the Time

For a more in-depth look at bestseller lists and the pros and cons of aiming for bestseller status, take a look at the two web articles by Max Tucker in "Further References."

Chapter 28

INSIDE A BOOK LAUNCH WITH CATHY FYOCK
AND LOIS CREAMER

What does a good prelaunch book campaign look like? What does it take to have a good first month?

Co-Speaker Authors and book marketing experts Cathy Fyock and Lois Creamer had just come to the end of their first month with their new book when I asked them these questions.

The Speaker Author: Sell More Books and Book More Speeches is 30,000 words of mostly short, easy-to-digest ways to combine book selling and professional speaking to the benefit of both. Their book shares their favorite secrets and best strategies using social media, email, personal appearances, newsletters, promotional paraphernalia, and more

One lesson I took away from reading it is that you have so many possible ways to sell more books that you will never do them all. So just do a lot of them, do them repeatedly, be creative, and have fun. Their book launch exemplified this strategy.

"Launch was great!" Lois began. "Cathy and I reached out to our databases with emails. We flooded social media with posts on all platforms. Cathy excerpted posts from the book that we could use in newsletters and guest blogs. She created pull-quotes from the book and turned them into seventy-five memes that we posted on LinkedIn, Facebook, and Twitter. We created bookmarks to give away when we speak. At the risk of sounding naïve, things went well, probably because of Cathy's expertise!"

"As soon as the book was launched," Cathy added, "I sent books to all those who provided us with testimonials and asked them to post selfies holding the book. I have been collecting these pictures and have used these individually and as a composite picture on social media. ('What do all these Speaker Authors have in common?')

"Then I sent them an email and thanked them for their quotes. I included their quote and a link to the book's Amazon review page and asked them to cut and paste their testimonial. I've posted messages on social media thanking people for their posts and highlighting the number of reviews. My philosophy: Putting spotlight on my clients/authors is the best way to benefit me."

The Year of the Speaker Author

Their premise in *The Speaker Author* is that authors sell more books if they are speakers and speakers get paid better if they are authors. To promote that idea throughout the year:

- They designated themselves and their clients as "Speaker Authors."
- They designated 2019 "The Year of the Speaker Author."
- They invited other authors to take pictures of their books and post them with the hashtag #SpeakerAuthor."
- They gave away buttons that said "I am a Speaker Author."
- They launched a year-long "Celebration of the Speaker Author" campaign that featured authors, their books, and a tip from each based on what they did as Speaker Authors.
- They created an "As Seen in The Speaker Author" social media campaign, which featured authors and their books that had been highlighted in the book, and these ran on the same social media channels.
- They created a template for LinkedIn that says "I am a Speaker Author" that, Cathy said, "we are offering to individuals who want to claim their authority!"

Debuting at Influence '19

Most important, they say, start early. "We started months before the book came out with strategy calls and assigning tasks," Lois recalled. "A big part of our rollout was to have the book before Influence '19."

Influence is the name of the annual summer conference of the National Speakers Association. It is the largest conference of the year for NSA members attracting members from all over the world. Influence '19 was held in Denver, Colorado, from Saturday July 27 to Tuesday July 30, 2019.

So, Cathy and Lois made July 1 their official launch date and tied their first month into the conference.

- On Monday July 29, as their first month drew to a close, they shared their ideas on how to sell books before, during, and after a speech with a full room at Influence '19. Their ninety-minute breakout session was titled "The Speaker Author: Selling More Books and Booking More Speeches," not accidentally the same title as their book.
- The content of their presentation was pulled from their book, which gave them the opportunity to refer to it throughout the presentation without being sales-y, a practice that is rightfully discouraged in NSA.
- "We weren't allowed to overtly promote. We couldn't sell books –that was being done at the bookstore," Lois explained. "We did read from the book so the audience saw it."
- "We encouraged folks to join our tribe and we'll continue to stay in touch with them," Cathy added. "At the end of our talk, we encouraged individuals to buy our book in the convention bookstore, and sold out immediately following our presentation."

A launch party that they co-sponsored that evening was the symbolic culmination of the first month.

After the First Month

And that's it?

No, that's just where a symbolic period comes to an end. Book promotion doesn't end after launch.

For Cathy and Lois, speaking is a major part of their ongoing promotion. Individually throughout their book's first year, they spoke at several NSA chapter meetings. In September, Cathy, a resident of Kentucky, celebrated in Louisville with her in-town friends, authors, clients, and prospects in conjunction with a writing retreat she led.

Together they taught a series of webinars and podcasts with their NSA colleagues and launched a new webinar devoted to the contents of the book

They did guest podcasts on the book and their business for Master of Ceremonies Warwick Merry from PSA (Professional Speaking Association) Australia; were interviewed together on podcast by brand marketing expert Amber Hurdle; and co-hosted a webinar with legendary speaker Patricia Fripp

Cathy began devoting a segment of her work to Speaker Authors once they have completed their manuscripts. Lois spoke to chapters of Canadian Association of Professional Speakers (CAPS), and PSA London.

Looking Back

In looking back, both Lois and Cathy affirm their launch campaign's success

According to Lois, "I think it went very well and give much of the credit to Cathy! Pre-work pays off! Start planning on time to put out prelaunch publicity."

For Cathy, the book allowed her to "continue to brand myself as The Business Book Strategist and to help authors leverage their books once written. Since I continue to receive inquiries for my work as a coach, this book has been a huge success."

A secret tactic was their successful collaboration.

"I like collaboration. Writing is lonely, and it's fun having a co-author," says Cathy. "I did the initial writing, then handed off the manuscript to

You've Got the Time

Lois for her additional comments, stories, and other advice. This worked out great, since I am more of the writer. In promoting the book we had no differing strategies or battles. We agreed to share the costs for producing and promoting the book, and we share in the book's proceeds."

"It was wonderful!" Lois adds. "Since we worked together before, I knew Cathy would be a great partner. We had no problems!"

"What's interesting about working together:" Cathy concludes, "Some things are twice as easy, others twice as hard. You have to talk about every big idea. Sharing our work was beautiful."

Look for Synergy

As editor of *The Speaker Author*, I was happy to use their launch to promote the first edition of this book, which was still seven months away from publication at the time of Influence. By doing so, I helped them to get the word out about their book. We had what folks in NSA call "synergy."

Having already determined my release date to be February 2020, I was more than three months away at the time of Influence '19. Kindle, where I print my soft covers, prohibits preorder campaigns for books that are more than three months away from publication. However, Smashwords allows preorders on its ebooks one year out. In fact, they encourage it as a book promotion strategy (see "Selling Ebooks: An Interview with Smashwords Founder Mark Coker").

So, I created a postcard offering 25% off the list price for preorder purchase of my ebook. On the back, I included testimonial quotes graciously given to me by both Cathy and Lois. I made sure everyone who received a postcard at Influence '19 saw their quotes so I could casually mention that I was their editor. I don't know if I sold any ebook preorders as a result of that campaign but I met lots of members, had the opportunity to answer their book questions, and picked up a few clients.

Meanwhile, I helped to get the word out about *The Speaker Author*. A common response: "Oh, Cathy and Lois have another book!"

Chapter 29

AN EXERCISE IN STRESS RELEASE

Okay, timeout. Think strategy. Your book is in pre-production. You've got good news you want to share with your fans but where do you release it?

Soon you'll have so much good news to share with your fans, you already don't know where to begin, and how do you tell your story in your words and your voice?

You start to feel stressed. So much good news. No way to get it out.

I've been there. Here's what you do:

1. Touch fingertips and heels of your open hands, fingers spread, elbows extending outward.

2. Now flatten your hands and press them into each other until you feel the warm blood flowing to your shoulders.

3. Now release the pressure, fingertips and heels still touching.

4. Now press again. And release.

5. Press. Release.

6. Press release.

7. Press release

Ah, feel the mental relief as the brain congestion caused by withholding news about your book from your fans begins to find focus in your next press release.

When to Write Press Releases

This chapter is an ode to the press release, your key to free publicity. Some call it a media release to include video and other digital media; others call it a news release. For most journalists and PR experts, "press release" is the search term of choice.

Press releases

- tell your story in your words,
- emphasize the points you want to share publicly,
- introduce your voice through colorful personal quotes,
- show off favorite testimonial quotes,
- provide the metadata to sell your book,
- instruct readers to take your desired action, and
- include your contact information so editors can get back to you for an interview.

They live forever in the e-world when you post them on your website. Be sure to use any keywords that will bring your potential readers to your site.

All in 350 to 500 words on one or two pages.

When you learn to write a press release, you can generate favorable news coverage for any one or more of the following occasions:

- After you upload your POD files, your ebook files, and your audio book files
- When preorders are available for purchase
- To announce your book's release in each version: soft cover, ebook, hard cover, audiobook
- When your book goes live on a new platform
- When you release a new edition
- To announce, then report on pre-publication promotions

You've Got the Time

- To announce, then report on post-publication promotions
- Before and after you make public appearances as author expert
- When sales hit milestone totals
- When you win awards, including bestseller status
- When an article you wrote appears in a prestigious publication (Thank you, marketing expert and press release advocate Lois Creamer, for this idea.)

And more.

A Timely Form of Barter

Press releases are a timely form of barter. Newsrooms are no longer flush with reporters. Today, newsrooms are more commonly understaffed and news budgets are underfunded. When an overworked editor is looking to fill six column inches by midnight with interesting content but no budget to pay a freelance writer, your well-written press release exactly fits the need.

Remember to include an electronic photo of yourself and another of your book cover.

On your end, although they don't pay you for the story, you get free publicity and goodwill.

It's a win-win.

You play the "local author" angle when you send your press release to media from the town where you were born, the town where you grew up, or the town where you live now. You can play the angle for the town where you spent a significant period of time or the town where a memorable event happened while you were there.

While you're at it, send press releases to the high school and college where you graduated and any organization where you can claim membership.

If you can find a local angle, exploit it because local papers love it.

Look for current events that relate to your book and comment on them publicly. Make the focus of the press release the event but then quote yourself and list yourself as "author of [your book]."

When you comment on issues of the day, people listen — because you're an author, which is two-thirds of "authority." What's the other third? You believing in yourself.

Where to Post Press Releases

Be ambitious in distributing your press releases. You have so many avenues.

- You can post them on your blog as news stories.
- You can post them on the book page of your website.
- You can upload them to free press release sites or a press release distribution service (see below).
- Sales expert and professional speaker Lois Creamer believes "the web is inundated with them." Even so, she suggests "posting them on your website under a section marked 'News' or 'Press Room'" where "they will get read and be seen by prospects who are checking you out."

Once they're online, they remain there forever. Use the keywords that the readers you want to attract are most likely to use.

- You can email them to your fan base and media list, including bloggers who review books and reporters who have written stories on similar topics.
- You can hand them out as flyers.
- You can stack them on information tables at conferences.
- You can leave them on store counters next to the cash register.
- You can report on your social media sites any time a press release gets published and then connect to wherever it was published.
- You can include hotlinks to your blog or website posts in your email signature.

208

Newspapers and magazines often reproduce press releases in their entirety. Sometimes they only keep one paragraph or reword your announcement to make it appear as their own original story. Let them play. It's all free publicity for you. Sometimes they even give you the byline, and you can include your book title and URL in your brief bio.

At other times they use the press release information as background material only, and then call you to do a full-scale profile interview. Good work. Those are the most fun to do.

Announcements about upcoming events may not be published verbatim but the vital information gets included in the community calendar.

Whenever the press release results in publication, drop a note of thanks to the writer if you can.

And even when editors don't publish your release, they may keep it on file so when they are looking for an expert who fits your credentials they call you. Here's what happened to marketing expert and book coach Cathy Fyock, co-author with fellow National Speakers Association member Lois Creamer of *The Speaker Author: Sell More Books and Book More Speeches:*

> One of my biggest breaks early in my career came when I sent press releases to a Human Resources publication (that was my expertise), and my short release was picked up. In a subsequent month, the publication was doing a feature related to my area of expertise, and a reporter called and did an interview with me. I was the only consultant noted in the article and, as a result, I picked up two instrumental speaking engagements which led to follow-on business. I'm a big believer in the power of press releases!

If you don't want to write your press releases yourself, you can find a freelance writer to do it but add a line item to your budget because good press releases aren't cheap. As a freelance writer, I made a lot of money writing good press releases for others and it was well deserved.

How to Write a Press Release

Here are the parts to include in your press release.

For Immediate Release

At the top left corner of the page, type in ALL CAPS:

FOR IMMEDIATE RELEASE

Headline

Skip one space; then write the headline, in bold type, centered on the line. A good headline should encapsulate the main idea of the entire press release in one catchy phrase that includes an action verb but excludes "a," "the," and, often, forms of "to be."

The headline should include the most important keywords from your press release. Some press release guides say only the first word and proper nouns should be uppercased but I uppercase all main words — meaning not articles or prepositions.

But don't get hung up on the headline already. You may not be able to write the definitive headline until you finish writing the body of the press release. In that case, use a filler headline that can keep you centered while you're writing the body text.

Dateline and Main Text

First paragraph begins with the dateline, the city where the release originated, in ALL CAPS; the state, as two-letter abbreviation; and the date: ANN ARBOR, MI, February 27, 2024 – ; or Ann Arbor, Michigan (February 27, 2024) – .

Following the dateline, the first paragraph repeats the main idea of the headline and expands on the main facts, described with a heavy sprinkling of keywords. The earlier they appear in your press release, the higher your search engine optimization (SEO) ranking will be, which means your story will show up sooner in Internet searches on more search engines. Use as many of the five W's and an H (or — Why not? — the 6 W's: Whow nice would that be?) as you can fit in.

The next three to five paragraphs put the event in its proper historical context or provide immediate background if your analysis is the purpose of the release. If the release is about your book, you can include bullet points to spotlight the benefits it will provide or share an overview of the content.

Write in third person.

As much as possible, personalize the release and the cover letter to it. Do your best to find the exact reporter who will care most about it. If you're focusing on the book, you may want the book review editor. If you're commenting on a related news event, you want the news editor. Do the research on the publication's website to find exact names and emails. Don't hesitate to make a phone call.

Remember: This is a news piece, not a puff piece. Keep to the facts and under 500 words. Under 400 is better.

Consider including a quote from a significant person to the story. If the release is about your book, you can quote yourself or include one or two testimonial quotes (each its own paragraph). If it's about an event where you will be appearing, you can quote an organizer of the event.

The quotes add color to the story but are often the first lines to be cut when space limitations intervene.

Author Bio

The author bio shows how interesting and authoritative you are. If you can fit in words like "award-winning," "bestselling," and "internationally known," don't let the opportunity pass. At the same time, don't puff.

Boilerplate

The final paragraph, called the boilerplate, is the "About the Company" template of metadata and contact information that appears in every press release. It tells what the company on the letterhead does and for what market, where you're based, and any desired combination of contact name, phone number, email, and website.

It also usually contains some phrase that exaggerates its importance: "the world's leading ...." Those phrases get edited out, too.

Keep the entire boilerplate to under a hundred words including your best keywords.

Contact Information

Write the contact information for the company representative you have designated to answer media questions:

> Contact name, title
> Phone, email, Web address

If you want to make your independent publishing company appear bigger than just the one-person operation it is, use a pseudonym as the lead person. Or use someone else's name. I use my wife's first name and her birth name; her title, President; our publishing company name, Azenphony Press; and my cell phone number.

Call to Action

Below the final paragraph, in bold type, include a "call to action." The call to action is what you want the public to do with the information you are releasing:

- "Order your POD or ebook today!" — with the website where they can be purchased appearing either immediately after the phrase or as a hotlink behind the phrase.

- "Enter today to win a free copy of [your book title]!" with the hotlink behind the phrase going to the entry form, an email, and a phone number.

That's All, Folks

End traditionally with "-30-" or "# # #" centered after the last paragraph. As a matter of style, years ago I started typing "kw" instead. I don't know if I ever had a press release refused because of that but I know I had plenty of press releases published so I don't think anyone cared.

Subject: Line

Use the headline of your press release as the Subject: line of your email message.

Posting Your Press Release

I use my company letterhead whether I plan to email the press release as a Word file attachment to a cover letter, my usual method, or pasted directly into the cover letter below the signature.

I do not use it when I upload directly onto a website form, the specified method of many media outlets.

Some experts say you don't need the letterhead when you send the press release in the email. Take your pick. It's a matter of style. No reputable editor is going to refuse your well-written newsworthy press release because you did or did not use your letterhead.

However, more and more sites have stopped accepting attachments because of concerns about viruses and security, an argument in favor of sending the press release after the signature.

The cover letter introduces either "the attached press release" or "the below press release" and gives a sentence or two about the content and why it will be of interest to the editor's readers, with your contact information so they can get back to you.

Some writers skip the cover letter altogether and just send the press release as an email. I prefer the personal approach whenever I can get it — hence the cover letters. Try both ways if you're undecided and evaluate your results.

Sending and Following Up

Standard wisdom says that Monday and Tuesday are the busiest days for press releases, which means you have the most competition on those days; and Friday is the day reporters are looking to the weekend and won't be paying attention; leaving Wednesday and Thursday as your best days to send releases. But many experts dispute that idea and say no day is the best.

However, most agree you should send your press release before 9 a.m. EST.

After sending your press release, if you were hoping to hear back from them but haven't yet after a certain period of time, forward the original message (which now either is still in your Sent: folder or has already been archived in the proper folder for easy retrieval). Urgency depends on timeliness. Will the release be too dated to publish a week after you initially send it?

In your new cover letter, begin with "Just a quick note to make sure you received my below notice and press release about [finish the sentence with a phrase that explains the release]."

Be gracious. Remember, you're busy but so are they. Assume they intended to get back to you and just haven't yet. Suggest that it got lost somewhere in the e-verse or swallowed up by the spam folder. In that way, you deflect blame away from them for simply ignoring you and you ease their guilt and defensiveness.

Goodwill goes a long way to creating long-term relationships.

I close with "Gratefully," and my name.

Don't hesitate to call a few days later if you still haven't heard from them. Ask if they received it and if they have any questions. Reporters, in particular for local publications, are generally accessible and they can tell you right away if they have any interest. If they do, tweak your cover letter to say, "Here is the press release we discussed on the phone today"; or "Here is the press release you asked me to resend."

MailChimp and Constant Contact

With email distribution, you can send it yourself to the names in your contact network or farm the task out to a press release distribution network to send to their network.

One way to send it yourself is to use an email marketing service. One popular service, in part no doubt because it is free at introductory levels and works well with WordPress, is MailChimp. Another is Constant Contact, which some say is easier to use and has nicer templates but is more expensive. In addition to helping you send press releases, you can use both services to send newsletters and automate your email marketing and lead-generation campaigns.

Following the on-screen instructions to set up an account on both services is simple. You can then import names and emails from your Excel spreadsheet of contacts.

Make sure to include all the media you've been meaning to add but didn't have names for. Visit their websites. Get the names. Most have either emails or phone numbers you can call to get the emails.

Both services provide tools to help you design a template that will further your branding efforts. The template can include your letterhead or a variation of it, your website colors, and other characteristics that you incorporate in the design.

Other tools:

- Emails can be sent to the complete list, segments of the list, or multiple lists at once.
- Once you submit your release, you can see which recipients opened your email and are worthy of follow-up to determine if they need a quote or more details.

215

- You can A/B split test your emails to see which subject lines have higher open rates.

But don't forget to perform quality control before you send out the release. Preview emails in both mobile and desktop formats. MS Outlook, I'm told, tends to blow formatting apart, so it's best to keep it simple if you anticipate many people in your audience will view through Outlook.

Press Release Distribution Networks

Years ago, when my marketing budget was closer to zero, I was fortunate that multiple free press release distribution networks were around to help me expand my personal media list. I placed press releases on as many different sites as I could.

However, I had little confidence that they were getting to anyone besides "Editor" or "newsroom@somebody.com." I had no ability to pinpoint my press releases to the exact readers who would be most interested in their general topics. And I was always irritated that for each site I had to make another tweak to fit their unique template.

So, for my launch for the first edition of *You've Got the Time: How to Write and Publish That Book in You,* I reserved funds in my budget to pay a reputable press release distribution company to help me expand my media reach.

Factors to Consider in Your Research

What are the factors that determine what to look for in a good network?

A study released in early 2019 by digital resource provider Fit Small Business rated over fifteen press release distribution networks on the basis of five factors: cost, word count, media outlets, multimedia types, and customer support. The best overall, as reported by Kristi Brown on the Fit Small Business website, was eReleases for its wide distribution and competitive pricing.

The eReleases representative who worked with me patiently guided me through the process and offered suggestions on my press release drafts.

The releases led directly to **one of my best reviews**, with *Midwest Book Review*. In fact, that review led to their doing **a second review** with an earlier book of mine. Another respondent brought me online to lead two Zoom workshops.

eReleases was founded in 1998 by small business advocate Mickie Kennedy. It reaches 90,000 registered journalists, 30,000 general media outlets, and more than 1,300 newspapers through the Associated Press (AP) News Network; and more than 4,700 websites, databases, and online services through its exclusive distribution agreement with the PR Newswire Network.

Included among the PR Newswire addresses, according to Kennedy, are "syndicated network partners that post most press releases issued.... Most of them are financial/business media sites that simply aggregate all releases."

eReleases offers three programs that range in price from $399 to $699. For first-time customers, they offer an additional 30 percent discount as well. All programs come with their media site-monitoring service, WireWatch, which enables you to track where your story gets picked up, which gives you valuable ideas for who to contact personally.

The more expensive ones allow press releases to be longer, offer better distribution, reach a more targeted audience, promise higher levels of placement, and accept more images and URLs per press release.

Authors who want to test the waters "should spend time thinking what their book offers readers and try to capture that in a descriptive and interesting way," Kennedy advises. "This is key whether working on marketing copy or an actual press release. Public relations is about refining and tweaking your message until you find something the media will respond to."

Authors who are planning major press release campaigns, he continues, "should realize that a campaign usually consists of three to six press releases. What can you say that is unique and newsworthy through a series of releases? You don't want to say the same thing again and again."
Releases are distributed before 9 a.m. Monday through Friday. You can schedule the date when your release goes out.

Other Press Release Distribution Networks

Other press release distribution networks recommended in Brown's article were Newswire, PR Web, Send2Press, PR Distribution, and PR Newswire.

Most companies, including eReleases, have some kind of template so they may have to tweak your releases to fit until you can do it yourself. Or, you can order writing services; for eReleases, the service is $300 for all three packages.

No matter which service you select, ask a company representative for suggestions on how you can find your ideal niche audience through their distribution network at a price that fits within your budget. Track the results using the software that they offer.

At the same time, don't sacrifice local radio stations and book stores. Kennedy agrees:

> If you were to call most local book stores and ask to do a book reading event on their slowest day of the week, most will say yes even if they don't carry your book, especially if you highlight that you will promote it online and on social media. Take advantage of social media and local media event calendars, as well as local groups – both online and off – to get people to your reading.

Bottom line: The best press release in the world won't do you any good if it doesn't get distributed. Start with your own media list, your blog, your website, and your social media.

Beyond that, reputable press release distribution networks are available to help you extend your message. Do your research.

The article by Kristi Brown referenced in this chapter and Mickie Kennedy's ebook, *Beginner's Guide to Writing Powerful Press Releases*, are cited in "Further Resources" and may be found online.

Chapter 30

SELLING EBOOKS: AN INTERVIEW WITH SMASHWORDS FOUNDER MARK COKER

You can't sell ebooks out of the trunk of your car. They don't work as back-of-the-room sales. So, what's the best way to increase your ebook sales? Mark Coker, founder of Smashwords and now chief strategy officer at Draft2Digital, has a few ideas.

Smashwords is the ebook distributor that, along with Kindle, has traditionally sold most of my ebooks. I liked their author-friendly philosophy and the tools they provided at the Smashwords Store to help authors publish, distribute, manage, market, and sell ebooks.

When Smashwords merged with Draft2Digital, Smashwords users suddenly gained the ability to create softcovers. Now, I had an alternative to Kindle. This was a huge benefit.

What D2D users gained was access to the legendary tools of the Smashwords Store.

A Few Free Tools

To name just a few:

- Your author profile page lists all your ebooks with hotlinks behind them that take you to an individual page for each book. You can post your bio, picture, and Smashwords interview; and connect to Facebook and Twitter, your blog, and your YouTube videos. Reviews you write of other Smashwords books will show up on your page, while readers who "favorite" you connect your page to theirs.

Readers can sign up to receive automatic notices whenever you release a new book.

- Coupon Manager allows you to create coupons that

  ◊ are automatically merchandised in the Smashwords Store:
  ◊ you share with your fans and reviewers;
  ◊ expire after the first x number are redeemed; and
  ◊ work across your entire catalog of ebooks.

  Custom coupons can be presented on your email list, website, blog, social networks, or printed business cards. They can promote exclusive "special deals" available only at Smashwords. You can give them to anyone who signs up for your private email list or reviews your book and they may be offered at a special price (including for free) to anyone who purchases the POD version of your book.

- Daily Sales gives you an at-a-glance-view of how your book sales are trending across different sales channels, along with detailed and downloadable sales reports that enable you to compare sales among retailers.

And then there's the tool that Coker proclaims his favorite easy-to-implement idea that most authors ignore or don't know about: the ebook preorder.

"Based on our data, fewer than 20% of authors take advantage of preorders," he laments during our informative email interview. "This is unfortunate because the small fraction of authors who do release their books as preorders earn significantly more sales."

With a preorder campaign, you announce that the ebook version of your book will be available for sale on Smashwords at a certain date but "If you buy now, you will save 25% off the cover price" or some such promotion to attract early, cumulative sales. The moment your book goes live on Smashwords, the preorders are fulfilled and your account shows huge opening-day sales.

You can put your book on preorder twelve months in advance of launch date.

Smashwords Book Marketing Guide

The free tools, including preorder campaigns, are spelled out in *Smashwords Book Marketing Guide*, written by Coker and available for free download at their website and all major ebook retailers. Coker refers me to it often during our informative email interview.

The book only has three sections but each section is a goldmine of information on its main subject.

1. 25 free book marketing tools available on the Smashwords website

2. 65 marketing tips covering five areas each of

   • Foundation building: author brand building, knowledge building, platform building, distribution, and autopilot marketing

   • Book promotions: prelaunch, blog, launch, library, and post-launch marketing

3. deep dives into the topics of social media strategies for Twitter, Facebook, and LinkedIn; how to work with beta readers; and how to earn free press coverage

"In addition to our self-serve promotional tools," he notes, "we actively promote selected titles to the merchandising managers of major retailers." The *Smashwords Book Marketing Guide* explains the criteria for selection.

The latest edition, which came out in 2020, "focuses on evergreen best practices that should work as well five years from now as they do today," says Coker. "Master the foundational basics before you transition to the shiny objects."

Distributing Your Ebooks with Smashwords

Smashwords, as part of Draft2Digital, is both a book distributor and a retailer.

- When you upload your book files to Draft2Digital, your book is listed automatically throughout the D2D distribution network, which includes Amazon, Barnes & Noble, Kobo, Scribd, Apple, Tolino, Overdrive, Bibliotheca, 24Symbols, Baker & Taylor, Hoopla, Vivlio, and Palace Marketplace.

- It also becomes available for sale at the Smashwords Store, the central repository for tools to manage and promote your books.

The secret to becoming a Smashwords bestseller, according to Coker, is to pay attention to all the sales channels because bestseller success depends on cumulative sales:

> The bestsellers you see on the Smashwords home page are ranked based on aggregate dollar sales across the Smashwords distribution network, as well as sales in the Smashwords Store. This means that your sales at Apple and other Smashwords channel partners contribute to making your book rise higher in rank within the Smashwords Store.

Give Away Your Books for Fun and Profit

And yet don't overlook the value of a new book given away for free. Coker is a staunch believer in the value of giveaways to get the attention of reluctant readers who haven't heard of you:

> By pricing a book at free, you make it easier for a reader to give your writing a chance. If you can hold the reader in rapt attention to the end, you have an opportunity to earn the reader's trust and admiration. Once the reader trusts that you're a great writer or subject matter expert, they'll be more willing to shell out money for your other books.

This strategy depends on your having a second book in you. Do you?

Of course, you do.

"Free works especially well for series starters," he continues. "It's a great opportunity to get the reader invested in your series so they're compelled to purchase the follow-ons."

Quoting Smashwords data that show free ebooks getting thirty times more downloads than ebooks at any other price, he concludes, "This means that not only are free books great at introducing new readers to your writing, they're also a great platform builder, especially if you advertise your social media coordinates and private email list at the end of your book."

But be real: "Do your own social media. Don't hire others to pose as you because such practices are disingenuous and inauthentic. Your participation in social media is a great opportunity for you to communicate directly with your readers, and for them to communicate with you."

Podcast

Finally, he offers his Smart Author podcast to help authors make their books "more discoverable, desirable, and enjoyable." The podcast is a step-by-step guide from the basics of ebook publishing to advanced best practices.

- It's available for free listening at all major podcast directories.
- At https://smashwords.com/podcast you can listen over a web browser or access complete edited written transcripts of each episode.
- The podcast offers a six-episode serialization of the *2018 Smashwords Books Marketing Guide*.

PART 6: SOME NOTES ABOUT BOOK CONTRACTS

Chapter 31

QUESTION THIS CHAPTER:
AN INTRODUCTION TO AUTHOR CONTRACTS

In an earlier chapter (see "Choosing Your Route to Publication"), I introduced you briefly to the traditional author boilerplate contract. The boilerplate is the version that the traditional publisher sends you and hopes that you will sign without question.

Unless you are an established author, a rising novelist, a criminal, a celebrity, or a politician, your boilerplate contract will stink, especially if it is with an academic press. The publisher's lawyers have seen to that.

But it's a lot worse if you go into negotiations in ignorance. You don't have to ever again, if you know in advance what to expect from your book contract, what the clauses mean, and what to do next.

In the chapters that follow, I introduce you to some of the most important clauses I have encountered in my over thirty-five years of being a book contract adviser with the National Writers Union's Grievance and Contract Committee — the brain trust of NWU. As contract advisers, we review your entire contract, teach you what the different clauses mean, and give you suggestions on how to negotiate.

Although not all of us are lawyers (I'm not) and we never claim to be giving legal advice, our combined knowledge of both book and journalism contracts is so vast lawyers come to us for advice. Writers often join when they find themselves looking at their first contract so that they can immediately ask for the services of a contract adviser.

Ken Wachsberger

As the founder of NWU's Academic Writers Caucus, I have been the foremost contract adviser specializing in academic press contracts, which cover anyone who is writing scholarly, nonfiction, technical, text, and other non-trade books.

What I have learned is that publishers assume their authors will blindly sign whatever publishers give them and, in fact, expect them to. Too often they're right, either because the authors are academics who are chasing the tenure truck and don't care about contractual nuances, or because they just don't know they can say no to a bad contract.

Remember: You have the right to negotiate the contract that your publisher sends you. Consider the boilerplate a suggestion. In fact, do not ever sign a boilerplate contract without asking for changes.

Ever.

And if the publisher refuses to negotiate, run as fast as you can and don't look back.

Always.

Chapter 32

YOU'RE SCREWED NO MATTER WHAT YOU DO –
BUT YOU CAN MAKE IT BETTER

In this chapter, I introduce you to some of the clauses that you are likely to see in just about any contract you negotiate.

Shoot high. Publishers won't accept every change you want but ask for it anyway. That's what negotiating is.

If you ask for everything you want, you don't get all of it but you get some of it. If you ask for nothing, you get all of it.

Seeking Your Input

After promising to publish your book at its own expense, the publisher will add a clause to the effect: "All details of publishing, including but not restricted to format, jacket design, pricing, and marketing strategy, shall be determined by the Press except that the Press may consult with the Author on these matters."

The key word here is "may." It is not protection to you. Cross it out and write "will." The publisher will object, especially about the right to determine price and format. You probably won't win that one and in most cases it won't matter to you. But you can counter by asking to separate price and format from jacket design and marketing strategy and keep "will" for the latter two. If you meet resistance, try "will seek input from."

In any case, absolutely do expect to move them in your direction. After all, isn't it sensible for them to ask you what selling points you think stand out and will make good cover copy?

Ken Wachsberger

The Worst-Kept Secret in the Industry

Here's a promise you don't want your publisher to keep. Not every publisher will tell you directly but they're all thinking it. It's known as the worst-kept secret in the industry: "Don't count on us to promote your book beyond listing it in the current catalog and sending out a few press releases and review copies."

Although they probably won't put you on tour, they certainly should send you an author's contact sheet where you can list academics who you think might adopt your book for classroom use, every journal you know of that might review it, and any other individuals or organizations that you think might review it on their blogs or purchase bulk copies; and then reach out to them when you send the list.

Suggest conferences and book fairs where the book should be displayed or where you should do signings. Find out how many review copies they are planning to send out and demand double, but have names for them. Remember, many review copies can be sent as PDF attachments.

Make sure they send you electronic copies of any press releases they write so you can reformat them on your own personal or business letterhead, personalize them if necessary, and change the contact information so responses come back to you when you send them out. In this way, you can make sales for yourself and the publisher from your own inventory (see "The Drunk Lawyer Clause"). They should see your action as you partnering with them, not competing with them.

Their promotion budget is based on the assumption that you, the author, have no interest in doing any of the legwork to sell your own book. Why wouldn't you? You care about the success of your book. You negotiated for a favorable resale clause that treats the publisher and you as partners.

On the other hand, if they do want to use you for promotion, make sure it is clear that they pick up the tab. For instance, your boilerplate may contain the following clause:

You've Got the Time

The Author agrees to appear in person at reasonable times and places upon the request of the Publisher.

If it does, insert the following sentences:

Publisher shall pay all related costs for lodging, transportation, and meals. Speaking fees will remain negotiable for each appearance.

Remember to initial all changes.

Image Permission

You will be expected to clear and pay for permissions if you use copyrighted photos, cartoons, graphs, or other images unless you can get the rights holders to give them to you gratis (surprisingly not as hard as it seems, especially for academic books). You also may have to pay for excerpts from certain text including lines from poems.

Here's how the clause may appear:

Permission: The Author agrees to procure promptly at his/her own expense the permissions which he/she and/or the Publisher deems necessary to reprint the material which is under copyright or to reproduce illustrations, charts, drawings, diagrams, or any other illustrative matter which is under copyright, should any such material or illustrative matter be included in the Work, and to transmit such permissions in writing to the Publisher with the final manuscript.

Yes, there is a concept called "fair use," which allows you to use a certain amount for free. The question is, how much is free and where does "too much" come in? The benchmark has never been strictly defined. If the rights holder wants to sue you for even a few words, you can fight it in court and win a legal victory but get stuck with court costs. You're always safer asking for permission.

If you know you won't have images of any kind, ignore the clause and save your energy for the clauses that matter. But if you will have images, calculate how much the permissions likely will total and how many books you will have to sell to pay for them.

Don't sign a contract whose best-anticipated result will find you in the hole. In such a case, insist that the publisher pay as many of those costs as possible, especially for images you don't think are important that the publisher insists on including.

Original Copies

While we're on the subject of images, a moment of mercy for the publisher here. Do not ever send the only copy of any image if you want it back.

Publishers always promise to return them, and reputable publishers do. But mistakes happen. Editors and image departments handle multiple books at once. Images get lost. You can express righteous anger at the publisher and the publisher will feel genuinely bad (because in most cases the "publisher" is really just an underpaid editor), but such expressions of anger and sympathy will not find your lost image.

But why are you sending an original in the third decade of the new millennium? Save yourself the grief. Send a camera-ready copy or an electronic file and keep the original.

Index

You also usually are expected to pay for the index (see "A Few Notes on Indexing").

Author Copies

You often can't purchase books to resell. Or they give you a modest discount to buy a minimum number and then deny you the royalty that you would get if a book distributor had purchased your book at the same discount and resold it (see "The Drunk Lawyer Clause").

You've Got the Time

Electronic Rights

Electronic rights used to be a 50-50 split at worst. Sometimes the author could get up to 90%. But that was when electronic rights were only a minor part of the income stream.

Then along came the windfall provided by the digital age. Instead of sharing it with the authors, publishers decided they wanted it all. Here's an example of what happened:

Around the turn of the millennium, netLibrary became the first ebook publisher of any consequence when they began negotiating with academic publishers to scan back copies of their catalogs to turn into ebooks. The cost to publishers to participate was two books:

- one for netLibrary to tear apart and scan
- one for netLibrary to display in their hard-copy library of print books they had turned into ebooks so they could show that the print and electronic versions looked the same

Participating publishers then turned around and offered their authors "appendices" to their contracts because "your contract doesn't have a clause for ebooks." In those appendices, they offered their authors 10% of net (15% if they were nice) for books sold by netLibrary.

They were deliberately deceptive. Contracts didn't have ebook clauses but they did indeed have clauses for electronic rights, and what can be more electronic than an ebook, which stands for electronic book?

"But ebooks aren't covered under e-rights," publishers conspired. "They're merely an extension of print rights." Writers' groups were slow in organizing around this blatant theft; likely no more than a handful of authors held out for what they deserved.

Today, new contracts routinely offer authors 10 to 15% net for ebook rights. Fight for at least 50%. This fight should not be seen as lost — but winning it will be a long uphill struggle. And, remember, you can say no to a bad contract and be your own publisher.

Leverage your power to walk.

Copyright

If you're not paying attention, they may take your copyright (see "Copyright: Keep It in Your Name").

Royalty

For authors of monographs or editors of essay anthologies, the standard for hardbound trade books is, give or take, 10% of list, or cover, price on the first 5,000, 12.5% on the next 5,000, and 15% thereafter. On trade paper, it's 7.5% on the first 10,000 and 8% thereafter. (Contributors to essay anthologies are usually paid a lump sum honorarium upon acceptance of the manuscript.)

The royalty you are offered for your academic book probably will be less for both hardcover and paper, and it probably will be based on net price, which means list minus expenses. Whatever you are offered:

- Insist on an escalating royalty structure rather than "7.5% on all books sold."
- Make sure royalty on subsequent editions is based on cumulative sales, which means total sales don't revert to 0 when your book goes into its second edition.

Still, the problem — besides the lower royalty — is that "net" is conveniently left undefined. Before you accept or reject any royalty offer, gather some hard statistics from the editor. Ask how many books will be printed in the first printing. How many of those will be sent out for reviews? (You won't receive any royalty on those.) What will the cover price be for the others?

How much of that price will be deducted before you get down to net, and for what reasons? Does it include printing, shipping and handling, discounts paid to distributors and bookstores, promotion, credits for returns, bad debts incurred during the royalty period, depreciation of equipment? What else?

The National Writers Union recommends that you avoid agreeing to contracts in which any expenses other than discounts and credits for returns get factored in. To the best of your ability, avoid deals in which printing costs and overhead are included.

Now you know on what actual dollar figure the royalty is based. Ask how many they expect to sell (in other words, before they come back to you and ask you to revise it). What will determine if they do a second printing and how big will that printing be?

Of course, they can't tell you the exact sales in advance. Every book has its own history. But they do have a pretty good idea of projected sales. That's the number you are looking for. That number times the dollar figure on which royalty is based will give you the best idea of how much you can expect to make from the book.

Now, what expenses are they asking you to pay? To obtain copyright permission for images? To format graphs and tables? To edit the manuscript? To create an index? How much will these costs total?

Do the math. How much can you expect to make from your book under the conditions they are offering?

Always keep this phrase on the tip of your tongue: "That seems a little low to me."

Second Edition

Publisher contracts often accept as a matter of faith that they can order up a second edition whenever they want and you will immediately comply. Or, if you refuse, they have the right to hire someone else to do the revisions for you and begin cutting into your share of the royalties.

Do you even want to do a second edition? You may not and the reasons why are your business alone, but their boilerplate contract assumes otherwise.

So, make your intentions known at the start. If you would be willing to produce a second edition, put regulations on the number of times they can arbitrarily require a new edition or the frequency of times, for instance, no more than once every two years.

Try for language that requires a new agreement altogether when the amount of revision is substantial, say, one-fourth or more of the original text. If that much material has to be changed, you're working on a new book. And if the first edition did that well, you deserve better for the second.

Hopefully you were able to negotiate an escalating royalty clause into your first edition, which means the royalty rate increases each time you reach a sales milestone (see "Royalty" above). That's great for the first edition, but if you didn't also negotiate a cumulative sales clause into your contract, all those sales will disappear in the second edition and you will start over at 0 sales.

If you would not, under any circumstances, be willing to do a second edition, cross out the clause, initial the change, and don't look back.

Royalty Statements and Withholding of Earned Royalty

Every press has a clause that gives your publisher the right to withhold your royalty payment at statement time if the amount on the check doesn't equal or exceed an arbitrarily large dollar amount, often $50 or more. When the author doesn't receive a royalty check, the amount remains in the publisher's bank account, where it gathers interest for the publisher.

Often royalty statements are issued only once a year, which means that if you haven't cleared their earned income bar by statement time, your publisher profits from it for another year while you don't.

Contracts should have no need for this clause. It's time for publishers to upgrade their software. Modern technology enables them to calculate your current royalty with just a few keystrokes.

Smashwords uses Paypal to pay any royalty balance of $.01 or more. According to Mark Coker, founder of Smashwords:

> The financial tracking systems at Smashwords are all home grown, and then we use Paypal to transmit the payments. A couple years ago when we moved from quarterly payments to monthly, I asked my team to also start paying all balances, even if they were only one penny.

> It doesn't require special software, just a commitment to pay your authors in a timely manner. We don't like holding on to an author's earnings because it's their money not ours.

Why can't other publishers honor that principle and make that same commitment?

If you expect to make a lot of money from royalties, certainly push for two or four statements a year. The publisher might agree without a struggle since most authors don't pay attention to this clause anyhow.

If you do not expect to earn much in the way of royalties, save your energy for more important clauses, like making sure you have a good resale clause (see "The Drunk Lawyer Clause").

And try to lower the earned income bar.

Author Warranty

The publisher doesn't want to get sued because of your carelessness. Make sense?

So they insert an author warranty clause that looks something like this:

> The Author warrants that the Work contains no matter that is libelous, obscene, or otherwise unlawful; that nothing in the Work infringes any literary or proprietary right, copyright, or any right of privacy; that all the statements contained within the Work purporting to be facts

are true; and that any recipe or formula contained therein, if followed accurately, will not be injurious to the user.

I get it, and so should you, in principle.

But we live in a global economy. As soon as your book comes out, it will be available for purchase all over the world. Has your book violated a libel law in Somalia? An obscenity law in Iran?

You probably have no idea.

But you understand how the law works in the United States and, to the best of your ability and understanding, you haven't violated any laws. Right?

That's all you're saying when you insert and sign the following clause, right after "The Author warrants…": "to the best of his/her ability and understanding."

Indemnification

Not surprisingly, the publisher will want you to cover attorney costs if a legal judgment rules against your work. So, they write

> The Author agrees to compensate the Press for any loss, injury, or damage, including its attorneys' fees, that the Press may find necessary to pay in settlement of any claim or judgment against it by reason of any violation of copyright or other property and/or intellectual rights or publication of libelous or any other unlawful matter.

But if in advance of publication you allowed the publisher's legal team to review your book and they agreed that no part was libelous, obscene, an invasion of privacy, or a violation of any copyright or trademark, you shouldn't be held responsible if they get busted for one of those reasons. After all, you were willing to make any necessary changes upfront. It's too late now but why should you pay because the publisher hired an incompetent attorney?

Agree to cooperate with them in advance but refuse responsibility for any subsequent expenses relating to lawsuits brought in connection with the Work once it passes legal muster. Agree also to cooperate in defending against such suits.

Advances

The complete phrase is "advance against royalties." Once the royalties you earn on your book exceed what you received as your advance, you start receiving royalty checks. The general rule is that you should ask for as much of an advance as possible because — at least in the academic press publishing world — that's all the money you likely will ever see from royalties.

But even if you're well placed in academia and don't need the money to live on while you're writing your book, you know your publisher will work harder to promote your book when it comes out if they invest more in it before it comes out.

If you are in academia, your contract may ask you for a subvention, which is an advance that you pay to the publisher. Is the humiliation of signing a contract that is one step removed from a subsidy contract worth the prestige you will receive by writing a book that bears this publisher's imprint? Will you benefit in other ways to make up for the cash you pay upfront: tenure, speaker's fees, personal sales through the resale clause, a second book with a better contract? As long as you're paying money upfront, look into independent publishing before agreeing to pay a subvention.

If the advance is paid in one lump sum, make sure you receive it upon signing of the contract rather than upon delivery of the completed manuscript or upon publication. After all, the idea of an advance is that you need money to pay bills while you're writing the book.

If payment is in two installments, make it upon signing and upon delivery — never upon publication, which can be delayed for any number of reasons that are out of your control.

Whatever they offer you, if they offer you anything, it will be low compared to trade publishers. Ask for double.

Right to Dump You and Leave You High and Dry

This clause actually appeared in one contract:

> In the event of the eminent publication by another publisher of a Work that duplicates the material and/or substance/thesis of this Work, the Author and the Press will re-evaluate the feasibility of successful publication. The Press shall have sole discretion to determine if publication is feasible.

According to this clause, you can research and write three-quarters of the book, with all the time, effort, and financial outlay that work includes, and then find yourself with no contract. Although it is heartening that the author gets to participate in the conversation, all power lies with the publisher.

Cross out that clause and don't look back. If the publisher insists on retaining it, demand a nonreturnable advance — which, in all probability, your contract does not include.

As a fallback, still demand an advance but agree to refund an amount proportional to the amount of the book you have not completed.

Think bottom line and dignity.

Grant of Secondary Rights

Before you grant any secondary rights, ask which ones they will be actively exploiting and how they will be exploiting them.

For instance, if they don't have an agent in Hollywood turning their books into movies and they aren't actively turning print books into audiobooks, don't give them any form of performance rights.

You've Got the Time

Keywords and phrases to look for in searching for references to performance rights include audio (sound recordings), video, motion picture, multimedia version, television and radio, cinema, cassette, filmstrip, disk, wire recording, stage, movie, dramatic, public reading, adaptation, visualization, and recording. If you want to retain performance rights, you need to strike all related keywords and phrases.

If they say they do make an effort to turn books into movies or audiobooks, ask how successful they've been in the past and with which books. If they have not been successful, they should be agreeable to letting you retain performance rights. If they are adamant and you find yourself faltering in the face of their resistance, give them limited-time rights, say eighteen months.

Remember your bottom line. Most academic books will never be made into movies, but, then again, most trade books won't be either and the same logic holds. If the publisher has no intention of exploiting the right, the publisher has no business asking to license the right.

Copies of the Manuscript

The Author shall deliver two double-spaced printouts and an electronic file of the completed manuscript in a standard word-processing format.

This clause costs you a ream of paper give or take, wear and tear on your printer's cartridge or photocopying expenses, shipping and handling, and the cost to insure delivery.

And for what? No one edits books off hard copy anymore. Any editors who do likely haven't made the transition into the twenty-first century and aren't equipped to do your book justice.

Cross out "two double-spaced printouts and," initial the change, and don't look back.

Ken Wachsberger

Honoraria

If you are contributing an entry to an encyclopedia or an essay to an anthology, it is likely you will be paid by the word. Contracts don't even use the word "pay." Rather, you will receive an "honorarium."

Whereas trade journalists are still pushing for $1 a word and above and many professionals would not think of writing for less, academic authors seldom realize they can negotiate and as a result often take what they are offered without question. A typical range will be 10 to 15 cents a word.

Some presses offer merely the honor of claiming a byline. As with poetry anthologies, they may pay in copies of the book. In any of these cases, double whatever they offer to provide you and don't flinch.

If your contract offers pay *or* copies, strike the "or" and write "and." You may or may not get both if you are contributing to an encyclopedia; the best you can get may be pay and a photocopy of your contribution — but it doesn't hurt to try.

But if you are writing a book, you should get both.

Confidentiality

What better way to keep writers ignorant about general working conditions than by mandating that writers can't share terms of their contracts with other writers? If your contract includes a phrase such as the following:

> You agree to keep confidential and not disclose the terms of this Agreement except to your authorized legal and financial representatives with a need to know and then only for purposes of representing your interests under the Agreement.

cross it out, initial the change, and don't look back.

You've Got the Time

Complimentary Copies

Publishers are notoriously cheap with complimentary copies. Whatever they offer, cross it out and ask for double.

Manuscript Rejection Pre-Contract

Most contracts don't have clauses that pertain specifically to peer review but a few words about the process are in order because it happens with academic monographs (including textbooks and dissertations), essay anthologies, and encyclopedias.

Most monographs come to the publisher unsolicited, which means the authors make the first contact. Monographs may already be completed or they may be in the form of a query letter, which is a combination outline of the book and sample of the author's writing.

For a completed manuscript, if the publisher has no interest, it will be rejected outright. If the publisher has some interest, it may be sent blind to four to six outside content specialists, which means the reviewers don't know who the author is. They will be paid an honorarium to review it and submit comments, which usually take the form of answers to a formal questionnaire that analyze the content, credibility, and marketability.

Regardless of what they say, the final decision will usually be with the in-house editor who is handling that manuscript. In both cases — outright rejection or rejection after peer review — because no contract has been signed at this stage, the publisher is under no obligation to provide any comments or helpful suggestions for the author to bring the manuscript into publishable form.

Ask for them anyhow, including copies of the peer reviews (which may or may not come with names of the reviewers). After all, it is to the advantage of both author and publisher if an already completed manuscript can be made publishable through revision. Even if the publisher sticks to the rejection, studying the comments may help you improve your manuscript and find another publisher.

Ken Wachsberger

Manuscript Rejection Post-Contract

The equation changes once you sign a contract. Although the process of peer review with the finished manuscript will be the same, now if your book is rejected you do have the right to a detailed analysis of why it was rejected and what you can do to make it acceptable — if you had the foresight to negotiate such a clause into your contract: "If manuscript is determined to be unfit for publication, editor will provide author with clear list of reasons for rejection and explanation for how manuscript can be made acceptable."

Contributions to a collection of essays will be reviewed by the general editor, who likely was hired on a freelance basis, and possibly the in-house editor as well. Contributions to an encyclopedia may be reviewed by one of a team of associate editors and/or the editor in chief and/or the in-house editor.

Depending on the practice of the publisher and the terms of the contract, final decisions may be determined by any one of the reviewers or a combination of them. For you as the contributor, it is important that your contract have terminology that requires the publisher to provide you with specific instructions on how you can bring your manuscript into compliance with their standards if it is initially rejected.

You can take some comfort in the knowledge that publishers, who are usually working on tight deadlines, do not find satisfaction in rejecting a manuscript outright because it means they have to find another contributor, who has to then start from a blank sheet of paper and still meet the same deadline in less time. However, in taking comfort, don't assume that means the publisher will accept a shoddy manuscript.

Alternatively, if such a piece has been totally rejected and you are the authority who has been solicited to write the same piece but now in less time, know that the publisher's urgency gives you negotiating power. At a minimum, you might ask for a more respectable honorarium or insist on maintaining your copyright.

Return of Notes and Knowledge

It is not unusual to find some variation of the following clause in academic press contracts:

> The Author agrees that all research, photographs, and related materials and information developed during the writing of manuscript are the sole and exclusive property of the Publisher. At the conclusion of Author's duties under this contract, Author will deliver all research and related materials and information, whether in hard copy or electronic or other media, to the Publisher.

Strike it and initial the change. This clause puts an undue burden on you to keep track of absolutely everything. Do they own correspondence between them and you? Do they own your contract adviser's communication with you? Your midnight freewrites before you drift off to sleep? What about confidential interviews or interviews that don't result in quotes or usable information? If so, you have to be upfront with everyone with whom you communicate.

Also, as a freelance writer you earn your living by reusing your material in different forms, with different slants, and for different audiences as long as it doesn't directly compete with the book that is the main subject of your contract.

Practically, the publisher will never use most of the material; has no moral right to ask for it or prevent you from reusing it, especially given what they're paying you; and likely will never ask for it anyhow. But if you're curious, or if they object, ask how they plan to use it and insist on your fair share of the profits.

For instance, they might want to store the photographs in their image database to use in other books that they publish, or post them on their website. In that case, keep the copyright to your photographs and your right to determine how you reuse them, and let them contact you for permission whenever they want to use one.

You can negotiate the payment later depending on how they plan to use it: one-time print, ebook, large circulation or small, nonprofit or for-profit, database, website?

You should never be obligated to deliver photographs that they didn't use in your book unless they paid for the photographic materials and your time in shooting the photographs.

Option on Future Work

Imagine your book is your baby. You take your baby to the hospital to be born. But imagine now that the hospital says, "By allowing your baby to be born at this hospital, you agree to consider this hospital as your first hospital of choice for your next baby."

What?

But many publishers do just that. Here's an example:

> The Author grants to the Publisher the first refusal of the Author's next work suitable for publication in print and/or electronic form, and the Author will not offer such work for publication to any other publisher until an offer made by the Publishers has been considered and rejected.

You've got nothing to negotiate here. Just cross out the entire clause, initial it, and don't look back. If you like how they treat this book you may go back to them for your next. But let them earn your loyalty, not contractualize it.

Out of Print / Reversion of Rights

See if you can find the catch in the following clause:

> If the Press advises the Author in writing that it has become necessary to discontinue publication, or if the Press fails to keep the Work in print and decides not to reprint it or license its reprinting within 6 months after the Author's written request to do so, then the Author shall have the right to have the Press revert rights in the Work back to the Author (The Work will be considered to be "in print" as long as copies are offered for sale through normal retail and wholesale channels by the Press or its licensee.)

What's the catch? To begin, "normal retail … channels," a phrase hidden within the parentheses, needs to be defined.

The phrase used to refer to print copies in inventory in the warehouse. If inventory dropped below a certain amount, publishers had to decide if they wanted to do another print run, which usually meant ordering a large enough run to get a low per-unit price. The total outlay was significant even if the per-unit price was minor.

Then came short-run printing, which enabled publishers to run off small quantities at a time, yes, even as low as 1, and still get decent per-unit prices. Suddenly publishers could have no books in the warehouse and still be able to claim that they were in print and available for sale.

A second publisher dropped the pretense and made no reference at all to "in print":

> If within six months of a written request by the Author, the Publishers do not make the Work available for purchase in at least one English language edition, in any format, including copies manufactured on demand or electronically transmitted, then this Agreement will terminate, and all rights granted to the Publishers under this Agreement will revert to the Author.

In both cases, your book will never be considered out of print or unavailable for sale.

It's a tricky clause. Argue for the determining factor to be level of royalties earned over a certain period:

> The Work shall be deemed out of print if no royalty payment has been issued in two successive royalty periods, whereupon all rights granted herein automatically revert to the Author.

Editors

While contracts for editors of anthologies and encyclopedias will have some clauses that touch on similar issues as contracts for authors and contributors, a difference pertains to the additional tasks of editors.

Editors may or may not be expected to contribute individual essays to the collection. They will be expected to do some combination of the following tasks:

- Create the table of contents, including front matter and back matter
- Write an introduction to the book
- Recruit someone to write the foreword
- Write scopes for all the articles
- Put together an editorial board
- Recruit authors or suggest authors and provide contact information so the in-house editor can find them
- Review contributions
- Find or suggest images for the articles (line art, photographs, maps, charts, and tables)
- Review typesetter page proofs

To accomplish these tasks, they may be expected to

- Attend conferences
- Make phone calls
- Write emails
- Be competent in current technology

The intensity of the work is determined by the size of the collection, the length of time allotted before typesetter date, the ease or difficulty in signing knowledgeable authors who can meet your deadline, and the competency of the editorial board.

Tasks of the board are a subset of the editor's responsibilities and, in fact, may be identical but for only a portion of the complete book. On the other hand, some board members are chosen only because their names on the masthead lend prestige and credibility. If any members of the board fail to produce, the editor will be expected to pick up the slack.

Final responsibility rests with the editor.

You've Got the Time

A Few Final Words

Looking at your first book contract is not easy. Contracts are a mumbo-jumbo of deceptive, vague, and intimidating legalese. Don't let yourself feel rushed. Don't make any conclusive statements over the phone without first taking a day or so to think about the ramifications.

Practice saying, "Let me get back to you. I need to speak with my contract adviser." You can be sure your publisher will check with their lawyer. Why should you do any less?

It's true that many writers will sign poor contracts in exchange for bylines. But it isn't true that the moment you speak up your publisher will dump you. Publishers are under tremendous pressure to produce many books fast. This is a testament to the megabucks publishers stand to make from your knowledge and your labor.

But publishers still want to produce quality books because their reputations rise and fall based on the books they produce. While they won't give in to your every demand, it is a lot cheaper for them to let you win on a few clauses than it is to reject you altogether and find another writer, with a good book, who won't make any demands, in time to get the finished product into the next catalog.

Finally, always think of your bottom line. If you're willing to cross it, then you aren't negotiating; you're bluffing.

Every clause you negotiate for the better is a victory for writers everywhere.

Solidarity.

Chapter 33

NEGOTIATING YOUR BOOK CONTRACT

The most important part of negotiating a book contract is convincing yourself that you have the right to negotiate in the first place. Too many writers think they have to accept whatever a publisher offers or they won't get published.

You Have the Right to Negotiate

That is false. Every contract is negotiable. In fact, you should never sign a boilerplate contract without asking for improvements. When a publisher offers you a contract, that means they want you. They've already invested a lot of editing dollars into you to arrive at that decision. You are in your greatest position of power at this time and you can negotiate.

Most publishers, however, count on writers to sign away all rights, no questions asked, in exchange for a correctly spelled byline. Your approach should be just the opposite. Publishers' contracts are written by their attorneys to benefit themselves, not the authors. In order to get a deal that truly benefits you, you must be willing — and you must have the courage — to negotiate. Consider a boilerplate contract merely the publisher's opening offer.

As a rule, contracts from the academic press are worse than contracts from the trade press. But the line between the two is narrowing as academic presses create trade imprints. With only a few exceptions, every publisher is willing to negotiate and make concessions. If your publisher won't negotiate, think dignity before byline and walk away. You don't need them anymore.

Ken Wachsberger

Exploit Me, Please

The purpose of a publisher is to actively and fairly exploit as many of the rights that your copyright grants to you as they can.

Yes, here is an instance when being exploited for profit is good. If the publisher has an agent in Hollywood actively turning their books and articles into movies, by all means give them a chance to get your book onto the big screen. If they actively translate books or sell in the foreign markets, give them a chance to do the same with your book.

But if they don't have any track record in Hollywood or in getting books translated, you don't have to give them performance or translation rights. Just cross out references to each one in the contract and initial all changes.

During negotiations, some publishers may say, "No one has ever asked for that before." Don't be intimidated by this response. In some cases, the publisher isn't telling you the truth. In other cases, you will be breaking new ground for writers. For that, we thank you. Think solidarity.

Ten Steps to Successful Negotiating

I prefer to carry out my initial negotiating over email rather than over the phone. I find it easier, safer, and more empowering to type my requested changes directly into the Word file of the contract using Track Changes and attaching it to a well-reasoned, carefully written cover letter.

But prepare for encounters both ways. In my more than thirty-five years of contract advising for author members of the National Writers Union, I have encouraged a combination of the two methods, beginning with email.

With email contract negotiation, if your publisher sends their contract as a Word file, you type your questions into the contract at the points where they arise. You delete unfavorable wording and replace it with clauses that read exactly as you want them to appear in the final draft.

You've Got the Time

Use Track Changes so your changes stand out. Then return it attached to a well-reasoned, carefully written cover letter that gives your overall assessment. If they send you a pdf that you can't edit, handwrite your changes and initial all changes. Then scan the file and return it as an attachment.

- Email helps you to document and frame your conversation.
- You don't have to worry about forgetting a main point or being sidetracked before you get to your strongest argument.
- You start a paper trail.

But contracts can take place over the phone as well.

When negotiating your contract, whether via email or over the phone, consider the following steps as they apply:

Step 1: Self-hypnotize
Convince yourself you're worth more than the boilerplate contract or you'll never convince the publisher. Practice speaking confidently. Say these two lines to your publisher with conviction (practice speaking into a mirror before calling the publisher):

"I am a professional writer." — This is especially important for academics. You're not just an academic who writes or a writer who teaches. You're an academic and a writer, a member of two proud professions. You deserve to be treated with dignity in both.

"That seems a little low to me." — I can't emphasize enough how much that attitude will get you. Say it slowly. Then pause. Wait for the publisher to respond.

Step 2: Know Your Contract
If you join the National Writers Union, you can obtain a copy of the *National Writers Union's Guide to Book Contracts*, which includes far more information than I can give you here about writers' rights, standard industry practices, and unacceptable contract terms. Members of NWU's Grievance and Contract Committee consider it our Bible. Question every clause in your contract and find counterparts from the *Guide*.

Step 3: Get Contract Advice from the NWU

As soon as you join, request the free members-only services of an NWU contract adviser by sending an email to advice@nwu.org. The NWU will set you up with a contract adviser who will take you through your entire contract, explain what the clauses mean, and give you ideas to help you negotiate a better contract. Being able to tap into the NWU's contract advising network is one of the most valuable benefits of National Writers Union membership.

Step 4: Know Your Bottom Line

When negotiating, you seldom get everything you want. The idea is to improve your contract as much as possible through compromise. Don't be so rigid that you lose a potentially workable contract.

On the other hand, not every contract is workable. What are your bottom-line issues, the ones in whose defense you would rather walk than compromise?

One right you want to fight to retain is your copyright (see "Copyright: Keep It in Your Name"). Publishers can do whatever they want with your book — as long as you give them the right through negotiations — while keeping the copyright in your name, where it belongs.

You want at least an even split with electronic rights. In the old days, when electronic rights were relatively worthless, authors used to receive up to 90 percent royalties on them. Then came the electronic age. Suddenly electronic rights had so many potential uses, publishers' lawyers couldn't keep track of them all so they invented a new phrase to insert in the rights clause: "all rights not yet invented." And they reversed the 90:10 royalty split.

What else matters to you? Only you know.

Step 5: Start High

As this is a negotiation, your opening offer should be higher than your bottom line. You will never be able to negotiate up, but if you start high, you will have room to move downward to meet your publisher on some issues while still coming out better than if you had accepted the boilerplate contract.

Step 6: Prepare an Opening Script and Good Notes

The opening script for a phone negotiation is an adaptation of your cover letter for an email negotiation. If you're comfortable on the phone and totally primed for negotiations, maybe an exact script isn't necessary. But remember the value of a good first impression in setting the tone of your conversation. A script will help you to set the tone of the conversation and state your opening case without getting sidetracked. Write it down beforehand and practice repeating it until it sounds natural. Only then is it time to make your call to or accept a call from the publisher.

Don't wing it or rely on memory during the negotiations. Write down the points you want to make about every clause, including the first bids, the fallback bids, and the bottom-line positions.

Assuming you've already talked previously with the publisher and you're on a first-name basis (Don't ever sign a contract with someone named Sir or Ma'am), here's a sample phone dialogue to get the discussion moving in your direction:

> "Hey, Les, I'm calling about my contract. I have a few concerns before I can sign it." ["Concerns" is better than "Questions."]

> Your surprised publisher replies, "What's wrong with it?"

> You say, "I want to publish with you because you're a prestigious organization. But besides prestige and a small advance [if you are so fortunate], what do I get for my hard work?"

> Or, "I'm pleased that you want to publish my book, and I know that you have deadlines so I would like to get this back to you as soon as possible but I'm a writer [not an academic or a professional speaker who writes!]. I write words to pay my bills. You're starving me here."

> Or else simply, "Would you like to go clause by clause?"

When you've said what you want to say, stop talking. Let the other person respond. In negotiations, often the first person to break a long moment of silence loses.

Step 7: Take Notes during Your Negotiations
Note taking empowers you and it prepares you for the inevitable follow-up communications. Record dates of all phone correspondence, keep digital files of all letters you send through the mail, create a running Word file of all email correspondence, and write down the names of everyone you talk to, including receptionists.

Step 8: Don't Make Commitments during Your First Conversation
Take a day to think about your phone conversation before making any commitments. Don't feel compelled or pressured to make a snap decision over the phone. Let emails sit for a day before responding to them. Report back to your NWU contract adviser and ask questions. When you demand time to think, you are taking control. You also are allowing yourself to psych up and prepare a script if you need it.

> If, during your phone conversation, you are uncertain about a proposal from the publisher, simply say, "Let me get back to you. I need to speak with my contract adviser."

> If the conversation is not going well, tell your publisher you need to call back (use any excuse to get off the phone). Then regroup, connect with your contract adviser, work out your game plan, and restart your negotiations.

Step 9: Ask Questions and Get Answers in Writing
Ask the publisher questions about sections of the contract that you don't understand. Request examples of how these sections will apply to you and get the answers in writing. Be sure that any "side agreement" made with the publisher is enforceable. Get it in writing and make it part of the contract. If a publisher won't put a "side agreement" in writing, then assume the publisher won't honor that "side agreement."

Step 10: Be Prepared to Walk
Those writers who have no human dignity and are comfortable being stepped on can ignore this step. But because you've read this far, you demand respect. You've already determined your bottom-line issues in step four. If

the publisher can't respect those minimum standards, you can exercise the right and the courage to go elsewhere.

I'm grateful for my fellow NWU contract adviser Paul MacArthur, who helped me update an earlier version of this chapter.

Chapter 34

COPYRIGHT: KEEP IT IN YOUR NAME

I'm asked by writers why they would want to hold onto a copyright. A better question would be, why would they want to give it away? Copyright protection is so important to society's well-being and the continuation of our culture, it has a place in the U.S. Constitution.

> Article I, Section 8, Clause 8: "the Congress shall have power to promote the progress of science and to promote the progress of science and useful arts, by securing for limited times to authors and inventors the exclusive right to their respective writings and discoveries."

The Copyright Pie

When I used to lecture to academics and emerging writers about book contracts and copyright, as a member of the National Writers Union's Grievance and Contract Committee, I used to picture copyright as a pie. (I thank former NWU grievance officer Amy Rose for that analogy.) You can sell the whole pie for a fixed price. Or you can sell different pieces for different forms of publication and use: First North American Serial, performance, translation, electronic, paperback, foreign, reprint, technology not yet invented.

These rights themselves may be subdivided. For instance, contractual terms used to designate performance rights include or have included audio (sound recordings), video, motion picture, multimedia version, television and radio, cinema, cassette, filmstrip, disk, wire recording, stage, movie, dramatic, public reading, adaptation, visualization, and recording.

The moment you affix your original idea in a tangible medium of expression — writing, a sculpture, a musical notation — the copyright to the expression of that idea — not the idea itself but the way it is expressed — belongs to you. The same is true with a fact — a fact can't be copyrighted but the way it is expressed can be copyrighted. Generally, a title can't be copyrighted unless it is sufficiently familiar to the public to have "secondary meaning." You wouldn't want to call your book *Gone with the Wind*, for instance.

Once you have creatively affixed your idea or fact in a tangible medium of expression — you've written your poem on paper, for instance — it is copyright-protected. In other words, copyright is yours from the moment you begin writing your book.

The copyright remains yours until you physically sign your name to a document that transfers it to another owner. That means you can't give away your copyright by saying, "Here, you can have it." You have to sign it over.

But Why Give It Away?

But there's no reason to give it away. Don't let publishers intimidate you or tell you that it would be more convenient if you let them have your copyright. Whatever they want to do with your book — distribute it around the world, translate it, turn it into a movie, make it an ebook, reprint portions of it — they can do while you still own the copyright.

They probably won't even put up a fight. The first time I said I wanted to keep my copyright, my publisher said he had never been asked that before and would have to consult with his lawyer. I don't know if he was trying to scare me or bluff me out but, a week later, he got back to me and said I could keep it. I wasn't planning to settle for less.

Don't be scared to ask. Publishers are working on deadline. They have catalogs to fill. It's easier for them to grant some of your requests than it is to chase you away and have to find another. Think "bird in the hand." They've already invested a lot of time and money into bringing you this far. Do they really want to start all over?

It's called negotiating and every editor and publisher will do it for a good writer and to meet a tight deadline.

So, what do you do if the boilerplate contract says the copyright will be taken out "in the name of the publisher"? You cross out "the publisher," insert your name, and initial the change.

Don't get me wrong: Publishers won't accept every change you make. That's what negotiating is. But if you ask for everything you want, you'll get some of it. If you ask for nothing, you'll get all of it.

And if they insist on taking your copyright from you, start looking for another publisher.

Chapter 35

HOW TO REGISTER YOUR COPYRIGHT

If you publish through another company and you are successful in hanging onto your copyright, your publisher will then contact the Copyright Office of the Library of Congress to register the copyright in your name. If you publish independently, you will contact the Library of Congress and register it yourself.

In either case, make sure you do register your book. Registration is considered notice to the world that the work belongs to you. It gives you the right to take copyright infringers to court and collect any damages that result.

And the process of registering is so simple: Go to https://www.copyright.gov/registration/, set up an account, and register online. It takes twenty minutes.

In most cases, you choose from two forms: single author of one work ($45) and standard ($65):

- You use the single-author form to register one article, one nonfiction monograph, one essay, one novel, one poem, or one short story.
- If you choose to compile a series of articles or essays into a collection, you use the standard form. Your co-authored book does as well. The standard form covers most works including an original work, a derivative work, a collective work, or a compilation.

A key word is "collection." I was told by a friendly voice on the phone that my book, *Ken Wachsberger's Puns and Word Plays for the Job Seeker*, had to use the higher-priced standard form because each pun counted as an individual work.

Likewise, *Your Partner Has Breast Cancer: 21 Ways to Keep Sane as a Support Person on Your Journey from Victim to Survivor* counted as a collection because the journal entries in part two of the book counted as individual items in a series.

For a brief moment I thought, "There's no way they'll catch me if I use the single-author form." For just as briefly, I next thought, "But what a pain in the butt it would be if they did." I paid the extra $20 apiece for peace of mind that my applications would go through each without a glitch.

Meanwhile, *Never Be Afraid: A Belgian Jew in the French Resistance* required the standard form because I co-wrote the book with the hero of the story.

In years gone by, you had to mail two print copies of your book to Library of Congress along with a check for payment. Now you just pay online and upload your book files, one each for the main text and the cover. The instructions are clear; "You may (1) upload electronic files if the work meets the requirements; otherwise, you must (2) send the work by mail (do not do both)."

That's it. The copyright is yours, your work is copyright-protected, and now it's registered. Remember to include a copyright notice in each copy of the work.

If you don't want to register online, you can fill out Form TX and return it to the Copyright Office along with two copies of your book but make that check out for $85. You can see the Library of Congress prefers online registration.

If you have questions, call them at (202) 707-3000 or write to their help line at www.copyright.gov/help. In my experience, they've been helpful on the phone, always my first choice over the help line. You have to listen to a tape but then you will hear a menu of options. Choose 1, then 0 to get a real English-speaking person. To hear Spanish on the other end, hit 1, 0, and then 2.

Chapter 36

BANK ON THEIR 501(c) (3) STATUS

During the process of negotiating, get to know your editor. Make it clear that you see this relationship as a partnership even if they don't at first. And that you need book promotion funds.

Remind them that they benefit when you are motivated to sell books because your effort will make increased sales for the press. They should have a mindset that when you succeed, they succeed.

But, they reply to any request for better terms, we have scarce funds. They have a valid concern that you must overcome.

Here's how:

Many presses, especially in academia, are 501(c)(3) nonprofit corporations that can accept tax-deductible donations. If yours is one, make it clear that you want to take advantage of their status so you can raise money from supporters to promote your book, including travelling to conferences and events. Your publisher should have no reason to say no if they're treating you like a partner, not a competitor.

But, make sure any donations are earmarked for your book. Otherwise, they'll go into the press's general fund and you won't see any of it.

Find a contact at the press who will let you know when funds come for you — easy enough if you give them the names of friends who promise donations. The press can keep a record of income and outgo so you always know how much money is available for you.

Michigan State University Press let me do that when I published my four-volume Voices from the Underground Series with them. My contract didn't allow for any money from the press for travelling to conferences and events. But I was able to raise several hundred dollars for travel by soliciting donations from friends who were looking for tax write-offs that year.

Wherever I travelled, I had books with me. My biggest challenge was lugging a sufficient inventory of four separate volumes.

Chapter 37

THE DRUNK LAWYER CLAUSE

A number of years ago, I was the freelance editor of a four-volume set of books known as the Banned Books Series that were published by Facts On File, a major reference publisher. I was offered a modest advance — well, not too modest; it enabled my wife and me to make the down payment on our first house.

Facts On File Contributors Give Me Editor Royalty

But that's not the point I'm making. I was offered no royalty, just the advance, because that's how book editors were traditionally treated. I told my agent I wanted a royalty also. I knew it wouldn't be a major windfall; the writers deserved more for their efforts than I did as the editor.

But, I said, "I know who I am. When the book comes out, when I see my name on the cover" — because I negotiated that placement — "I know I'll be out there selling the book. My efforts will help the authors. My efforts will help Facts On File. I deserve a royalty."

And I got it. Of course, it was only 1% or so, and it came out of the authors' royalties (with their agreement) rather than from Facts On File. But I was pleased to know that, according to the publisher, I was the first editor ever to receive a royalty from Facts On File. And I did promote the book, to everyone's advantage.

But not because of the 1% royalty, which, in Yiddish, would be known as a *pitzelach*, a teeny bit.

Ken Wachsberger

Facts On File Sees the Logic

In the boilerplate contract was a clause, known as the resale clause, which said that the volume authors and I could purchase a minimal number of books, ten or so, at some modest discount, between 30 and 40%. But then the next phrase said, "but not for resale." The sentence after that said, "Royalties will not be paid on books purchased at author discount." This is a common clause in boilerplate contracts, especially academic press contracts, which are the worst in the business.

We know that boilerplate contracts are written by publishers' lawyers, and that the contracts are generally to the advantage of the publishers. But this clause was destructive to both the publisher and the author. I'm sure it was written by a drunk lawyer because it harmed his own client. It treated the contributors to the book as competitors to the publisher.

I said to my agent, "I want to be able to purchase books at 50% off or the best distributors' discount, for resale, and with no risk to my royalty. If Baker & Taylor purchases books at 50% off to resell to libraries, I don't lose my royalty. Why should I lose my royalty if I purchase for myself at 50% off?"

Further, I argued, I knew I would be walking into bookstores and libraries that their salespeople would never approach. I knew I would be setting up speaking opportunities on my own dime. Why should Facts On File get the money?

Fortunately, Facts On File was enlightened enough to see the logic. They allowed the revised clause. And I made it worthwhile for them. The set sold in hardcover for $140. Libraries loved the set. They still are a mainstay of Banned Books Month every year and have gone through at least two revisions.

Free Money All Around

For me, I would walk into a library, show the purchaser the set, walk out with a check for $140, and bank half of it. It was free money for the publisher because I found outlets their best sales force couldn't find. Facts

268

On File may have only made 50% of $140 but it was a lot better than 100% of nothing. And they did no better when distributors sold it. In fact, I was a distributor. That's how they related to me.

They treated me as a partner, not as a competitor.

PART 7: "YOU CAN DO IT" SECTION

Chapter 38

THE REWARD SYSTEM WORKS

The reward system is part of the process of writing, and it works.

My message to you is that you need to set modest goals along the way to your finished products. When you achieve any goal, give yourself a reward: a half hour of TV without guilt or a phone call to a friend after writing three pages.

Use the reward system not only to reward productivity in writing but to alleviate guilt if you think you should be doing something else — like earning a living. Unpack five boxes and write for an hour. Finish your taxes and write for an hour. You can't wait until you're totally caught up because we never get totally caught up.

I'm reminded of a lesson I learned around the reward system when my son David was seven-years old. The year before, we had bought him his first two-wheeler for his sixth birthday. It was a bright red bike that said "Team Murray" on the side and he loved it. He showed it off to all the neighbors. The only trouble was, he never rode it, at least not after his first few falls. He just refused to try. He even attempted to convince me — and, hence, himself — that he didn't want to ride his bike.

I was reminded of how I used to suck my thumb when I was around his age. My dad couldn't get me to stop and he didn't know what to do. Finally, one night as he was tucking me into bed, he said he would buy me a baseball glove if I could go a week without sucking my thumb. I never sucked my thumb again.

Of course, to this day I bite my nails.

Anyhow, David was into Nintendo by this time so I promised him I would buy him any Nintendo game he wanted as soon as he learned how to ride his bike. He was riding it the next day.

Today, David is a graduate of the Culinary Institute of America and an acclaimed executive chef.

The reward system works.

Chapter 39

THE ME-YOU-US THEORY

One of the most difficult periods of my long, happy marriage with my life partner, Emily, was when I was editing my Voices from the Underground Series, a four-volume collection of histories of individual underground newspapers — the independent, antiwar press from the Vietnam era — as written by key people on each of the papers.

I conceptualized the series while editing a family of library journals in Ann Arbor and contributed my own history of the underground papers from East Lansing-Lansing, Michigan, where I used to write. Then I sent my story to veterans of other papers and invited them to write similar pieces for their papers, to appear as articles in one of my journals.

Editing Four Books at a Time after Day Job

It had come out once in 1993 as an oversized, 600+-page book that was laid out in an 8 ½" x 11", two-column format, the content equivalent of four books. It had few images so it was dense with copy. This new edition broke the complete original collection of stories plus three new stories into a series of four separate books, which all had to be updated. Stories were rich with photos and images that all required copyright clearance. It was the most intense, concentrated period of freelance editing and permission gathering I have ever experienced.

I had a full-time job at the time, also as an editor. I drove a long way on several connecting freeways from Ann Arbor into Farmington Hills, a suburb on the northwest side of Detroit, to be underpaid and disrespected. I had to psych myself up every day to get through the day.

While I was working on Voices, I arrived in Farmington Hills two hours early and edited at the Panera down the road from the company. At the end of my work day, I'd return to Ann Arbor and stop at the Panera that was on the route to my home to edit until closing.

By the time I got home most nights, Emily was in bed and about to turn off the lights. I'd kiss her. We'd share about five minutes of our respective adventures for the day. Then she'd go to sleep and I'd grab a late dinner.

I put in as many hours as I could on weekends.

You don't have to warn me that such behavior will stress out even the best of relationships.

Emily was my hero during that time because she gave me the space I needed to do what I had to do to finish four books at the same time. To my credit, I had early on in our partnership begun preparing her for this very situation.

A Theory Is Born

Here's what happened: When I first realized that Emily was going to be a major part of the rest of my life if I didn't screw up, I introduced her to my Me-You-Us Theory, which states that a successful relationship includes three partners: the Me, the You, and the Us; and each has to be fed regularly to keep them all healthy.

A corollary states that at any one time, one may dominate and the others will have to adjust. I was in my Me, and Emily trusted that I would come back.

On my part, I was always aware that Emily was missing me. I was missing her, too. So, I worked harder to support the You when we were together which had the desired effect of making the Us stronger. I saw whatever movies she wanted to see, ate at the restaurants of her choosing, or stayed in and watched TV if that was her mood for the evening.

Mostly we went out with each other but no one else, to reconnect. When we socialized, Emily often spoke for me because, even though I was present in the physical plane, my mind was elsewhere. I can shut down my laptop but I can't always shut down my mind, even for small talk.

The Voices from the Underground Series put the Me-You-Us Theory to the test and I can say that it is a good theory; but it takes a lot of effort and trust on the part of both partners to make it work. Because there will come a time in your relationship with your book when it becomes possessive and demanding of your time.

When your book starts to take over your life and you are afraid that you'll go crazy if you don't give into it, remember: You're in your Me. Tell your family members you love them and you'll be back. They'll understand. If they're like Emily, they'll take advantage of that time to pursue their own personal and professional growth.

Chapter 40

I WRITE A WRONG IN SYRACUSE:
THE POWER OF A WELL-WRITTEN MESSAGE

Writing is a powerful form of communication in this society. I know you agree. That's why you're writing your book.

In my own life, I've taken on the city of Syracuse, a window company, numerous landlords, Blue Cross/Blue Shield, and many others just by writing letters. Before I bring this book to an end, I'd like to tell you my Syracuse story.

Visiting Cousin Steven

Several years ago, on a vacation journey to New York City with my wife, Emily, and my one-year-old son, David, we stopped in Syracuse to visit Emily's cousin Steven. Steven and his family lived on the top of a hill. Although it was legal to park in the street, he advised us to park in the driveway because cars speeding up the hill often didn't see cars parked at the top. We followed his advice.

The next morning, while we were enjoying a breakfast of fresh bagels and cream cheese, we heard a knock at the door. Steven answered it. Standing on the porch were two men who worked for the city of Syracuse. The first asked rhetorically, "Does anyone here own the light blue Chevette?"

When I came to the door, he explained that their job for the day involved their transporting telephone poles from one location to another. Because any telephone pole that was standing upright in a truck would have little chance of remaining standing throughout the trip, they were wisely, in their opinion, laying them down in the back of the truck.

Unfortunately, the poles were much longer than the bed of the truck and so they protruded a great distance over the edge. While making a turn by Steven's house, one pole cut a curved path so wide that it bashed the right front fender of my poor Chevette.

"Don't Worry about a Thing"

"Don't worry about a thing," the worker told me. "We're insured by the city of Syracuse. Just get an estimate and send it in and you'll be reimbursed."

"But I live in Lansing, not Syracuse, and we're on our way to New York tomorrow," I explained to him.

"Don't worry," he said. "Enjoy your vacation. Just send us an estimate when you get back to Lansing."

So, after meeting with the proper representative at city hall to make arrangements for an estimate to follow, we headed off into the big city. The next week, when we returned home, I did as I had been instructed. I sent an estimate of $335.30 from the dealership where I bought my car along with a cover letter which said in part:

> Relative to my claim against the City of Syracuse for the incident of June 28, 1984, in which my car was hit by a city vehicle, enclosed is an estimate for repairs, as you requested.

> Thank you for your courtesy when I met with you in your office.

> I look forward to your immediate response.

Screwed by a "Compromise Agreement"

A month later, I received the following form letter from their Claims and Safety Division:

You've Got the Time

Dear Sir:

Enclosed please find a compromise agreement regarding the above captioned action. Kindly execute where indicated before a notary public and return it to this office.

As soon as the agreement is received by this office we shall present it to the Board of Estimate for their required approval. Payment of the claim is subject to their approval.

The key word here is "compromise." Their check was for $254. I was expected to cover the rest. How had I contributed to the situation, I wondered. Maybe I had put too much cream cheese on my bagel. Anyhow, it wasn't too difficult to realize that they were taking advantage of my being from out of state. According to my way of thinking, they figured I wouldn't want to make a big deal out of it. What was I going to do, hire a lawyer? Take them to court in Syracuse? For 80 bucks?

They didn't know I was a writer, an investigative reporter, and a researcher. Two months later, after doing my own research into the matter, I wrote the letter writer the following letter:

Relative to your insulting form letter of August 16, 1984 (Xerox enclosed): I am not interested in what you call "a compromise agreement." What does that mean: You will offer me some of the money I need to repair my vehicle and I have to pay the rest myself?

On June 28, 1984, one of your drivers, Robert Culkin, smashed into my car. I wasn't even in the car. Furthermore, my car wasn't even in the street: it was in the driveway.

I had to leave town the next morning, so I sent an estimate in good faith from Lansing, Michigan, my home, as requested by Ms. Ellen Holmes of your office. You sent back an offer that does not cover the cost. I should not have to pay a dime.

281

I have discussed this with my lawyer.

I have discussed this with my Allstate insurance agent.

I have discussed this with the insurance commissioner.

They all agree. I should not have to pay out of my pocket for your driver's carelessness.

Enclosed is a copy of my first estimate and originals of two others [both were well over their "compromise agreement"]. Bud Kouts Chevrolet is the dealership where I bought my car. Pick your favorite but let's take care of this matter between ourselves rather than through the courts. The vehicle that your employee smashed is my business car and my business is not helped when I drive what looks like a demolition derby loser.

The City of Syracuse is clearly at fault. There is no question about that. Negligence has already been admitted. The only question is, are you willing to pay me what you owe me? Surely, if I owed the City of Syracuse taxes, you would expect payment. Now you owe me. Why should I expect less?

I look forward to a prompt timely reply.

The year was two weeks short of ending when I received the following reply, from the assistant claims officer:

Dear Mr. Wachsberger;

I refer to your letter of 10-25-84. Our file with your letter was referred to Corporation Counsel Attorneys for disposition.

They will agree to a top offer of $275.00 to settle claim. If you are agreeable, please advise.

You've Got the Time

Seeking Redress from the Mayor

Would you have been agreeable? I got tired of dealing with bureaucrats and wrote the following letter to the mayor. In case you aren't noticing, each letter is getting longer. In addition, I included in each reply photocopies of all previous correspondence plus copies of all the estimates, so each package was getting progressively heavier. Here's the letter:

Dear Mr. Mayor:

I've been to your city one time and I believe I've been wronged. Where do I go for redress of grievances?

As you can see from the enclosed file of correspondence, my brief stay in Syracuse was marred when, on June 28, 1984, one of your city drivers, Robert Culkin, smashed into my car. It wasn't even in the street at the time — it was in the driveway.

But I'm not writing you to attack Mr. Culkin's driving ability. We all have off days. This was his, and he admitted fault.

I had to leave town the next morning for an appointment in New York City so, on July 19, 1984, I sent an estimate for repairs, in good faith, from Lansing, Michigan, my home town, as requested by Ms. Ellen Holmes of your Claims and Safety Division.

The letter from Frances M. Mooney, also of your Claims and Safety Division, dated August 16, 1984, offered what was euphemistically called "a compromise agreement" that fell far short of the estimate. The implication of a compromise is that both parties are at fault. I wasn't even in the car when it was hit.

In my response of October 25, 1984, I sent a xerox copy of my original estimate and originals of two others. I have enclosed copies for your enlightenment.

As you can see, they were all well above your first offer.

The latest letter in our exchange, from Dudley C. Breed, Assistant Claims Officer, dated December 14, 1984, tells me your Corporation Counsel Attorneys "will agree to a top offer of $275.00 to settle the claim." In other words, your city attorneys have offered to rip me off and are asking me to agree.

Of course I don't agree. Further, I believe I'm being deliberately ripped off and harassed because I'm from out of state. I've threatened to go to court if I have to — but is this the way the city of Syracuse does business? Isn't it enough that I have to drive around in a business car that looks like a demolition derby reject?

Isn't it enough that I had to take time out of my busy schedule to compile estimates to rectify damage caused by your driver?

Do I now have to pay for an injury inflicted upon me in partnership with the party that, by its own admission, is solely at fault?

Where are justice and fairness in Syracuse, New York?

And on which side of the line does its mayor stand?

I'm asking for your help, Your Honor, in collecting what is clearly due to me.

Thank you for your immediate attention.

Resuming Diplomatic Relations with Syracuse

When two weeks later I received a friendly letter from the deputy mayor informing me that he had been ordered by the mayor to look into the matter, I wrote him "a short note to let you know that I received your letter of February 7, 1985 and am most appreciative of both your quick response and your obvious concern. I look forward to a rapid resolution of this matter and a resumption of diplomatic ties with the city of Syracuse."

On March 29, 1985, I received a note from Syracuse's assistant corporation counsel, Robert Jenkins, indicating that they were prepared to pay me $313.15, which was equal to the amount of the lowest of the three appraisals. Bud Kouts Chevrolet agreed to repair my car for that amount even though their estimate had been higher, so I accepted.

After an exchange of a few brief letters to complete the transaction, I received the check and a letter from Robert Jenkins saying, "we hope that you will resume diplomatic ties with the City of Syracuse."

I did, but on my terms.

FURTHER RESOURCES

General

1. Coker, Mark. *Secrets to Ebook Publishing Success: How to Reach More Readers*. Los Gatos, CA: Smashwords (2014).

2. Coker, Mark. *Smashwords Book Marketing Guide*. Los Gatos, CA: Smashwords (2008-2018).

3. Curtis, Richard. *How to Be Your Own Literary Agent: An Insider's Guide to Getting Your Book Published*. Rev. 4th ed. New York: Mariner Books (2003).

4. Fyock, Cathy, and Lois Creamer. *The Speaker Author: Sell More Books and Book More Speeches*. Louisville, KY: Remarkable Books Publishers (2019).

5. Kawasaki, Guy, and Shawn Welch. *APE: Author, Publisher, Entrepreneur – How to Publish a Book*. Palo Alto, CA: Nononina Press (2013).

6. Levinson, Jay Conrad, Rick Frishman, Michael Larsen, and David L. Hancock. *Guerrilla Marketing for Writers: 100 No-Cost, Low-Cost Weapons for Selling Your Work*. Garden City, NY: Morgan James Publishing (2010).

7. Lutze, Heather. *Marketing Espionage: How to Spy on Yourself, Your Prospects and Your Competitors to Dominate Online*. Parker, CO: Findability Press.

8. Perlman, Corey. *Social Media Overload! Simple Social Media Strategies for Overwhelmed and Time-Deprived Businesses*. Roswell, GA: Garnet Group Publishing Group (2014).

9. Poynter, Dan. *Dan Poynter's Self-Publishing Manual: How to Write, Print, and Sell Your Own Book*, 16th ed. Santa Barbara, CA: Para Publishing (2007).

10. Tucker, Max. "How Bestseller Lists Actually Work — and How to Get on Them…." *Entrepreneur* (August 30, 2016).

11. Tucker, Max. "How to Get on the NY Times & Every Other Bestseller Book List." *Scribe* (December 18, 2018).

About Press Releases

12. Brown, Kristi, "6 Best Press Release Distribution Services 2019." (January 31, 2019).

13. Class: PR. "The 12 Best Press Release Distribution Services (2019)."

14. Kennedy, Mickie. *Beginner's Guide to Writing Powerful Press Releases: Secrets the Pros Use to Command Media Attention* (2013).

15. MacArthur, Amanda. "The Best Paid and Free Press Release Sites." *Mequoda Advice* (January 13, 2016).

Groups to Seriously Consider Joining

- Independent Book Publishers Association

- National Speakers Association

- National Writers Union

- Toastmasters

A FINAL WORD OR TWO

Thank you for purchasing and reading the second edition of *You've Got the Time: How to Write and Publish That Book in You.*

I learned a lot about writing and publishing a book while I was writing and publishing this book about how to write and publish a book. I hope you found reading it to be as enlightening and that you made major progress on your book along the way.

If you did, please be kind enough to post an honest review of *You've Got the Time* on your blog, through your social media networks, or at your favorite retailer so that other readers can find it. Then again, if you didn't find it helpful, go ahead and review it as well. (I just hope there are fewer of you.)

Writing is a solitary practice but writing and publishing a book is a team effort. If you would like to

- talk to me about coaching, editing, or speaking, or
- learn how to purchase orders in bulk for your classroom, organization, or business, or
- book me to speak about "Writing for Healing and to Preserve Your Legacy"

please contact me at
http://www.kenthebookcoach.com
ken@kenthebookcoach.com

Ken Wachsberger

ABOUT THE AUTHOR

Ken Wachsberger, The Book Coach, has been writing and helping others to write better, through personal book coaching and editing, for nearly fifty years, going back to his work on the underground press of the Vietnam era.

Under Ken's gentle guidance, students, clients, and friends have

- worked through personal traumas
- prepared for life transitions
- made major purchases, and
- chosen their life paths

while writing more than they ever believed possible, and better.

His landmark *Transforming Lives: A Socially Responsible Guide to the Magic of Writing and Researching* was the first textbook written to teach Ken Macrorie's I-Search paper.

While trapped in corporate America, he oversaw and edited some classic award-winning, multi-volume encyclopedias, including *New Encyclopedia of Africa* (5v), *Encyclopedia of Public Health* (4v), *Tobacco in History and Culture* (2v) *and Baker's Biographical Dictionary of Popular Musicians since 1990* (2v).

As a digital historical researcher, he conceptualized and created the most extensive open access, keyword-searchable collection of digital reproductions of underground, alternative, and literary newspapers and magazines in existence.

As a member of National Speakers Association, Ken offers group and personal book coaching and editing so speakers and others can write and publish the books they need for credibility and back-of-the-room sales. As a member of National Writers Union, he teaches members how to understand and negotiate book contracts.

He can be reached at ken@kenthebookcoach.com or http://www.kenthebookcoach.com.

BOOKS BY KEN WACHSBERGER

Available as PODs and ebooks

- *You've Got the Time: How to Write and Publish That Book in You,* 2nd edition

- *Your Partner Has Breast Cancer: 21 Ways to Keep Sane as a Support Person on Your Journey from Victim to Survivor*

- *Never Be Afraid: A Belgian Jew in the French Resistance,* 3rd edition

- *Ken Wachsberger's Puns and Word Plays for the Job Seeker*

Upcoming in POD and ebook:

Beercans on the Side of the Road: The Story of Henry the Hitchhiker, considered a cult classic when it was first released in print in 1987

OTHER BOOKS BY KEN may be found at

http://www.azenphonypress.com

http://www.voicesfromtheunderground.com

Printed in the USA
CPSIA information can be obtained
at www.ICGtesting.com
JSHW021032080823
46148JS00002B/123

9 780945 531210